P9-CEN-449

Endorsement

Jim Kouzes, coauthor of the bestselling books *The Leadership Challenge* and *Credibility*

"As Peter Alduino makes clear in *The Citizen Leader*, leadership is not about position or title, power or authority, celebrity or wealth. And it's most definitely not about being a hero. What Peter says is that leadership is your responsibility as a member of this global community, and that you have the capacity to do it. When you read *The Citizen Leader*, Peter asks you to confront yourself, take stock of who you are, and what you stand for. And he asks you to decide the difference you want to make in this world. This book is full of tips and techniques and practical examples, and all the things you need to become a better citizen leader, but it is not a book you just read, it's a book you have to experience. It's a book that you have to actively participate in. When you do, it will affirm the most fundamental of all assumptions that you must make to become an exemplary leader — the assumption that you make a difference. *The Citizen Leader* will help you do just that."

THE CITIZEN LEADER

BE THE PERSON YOU'D WANT TO FOLLOW

Peter Alduino

Copyright © 2011 by Bridge Group Communications, LLC.
All rights reserved. No part of this work may be reproduced, distributed or transmitted in any form or by any means, electronic or mechanical, including photocopying and recording, or by any information storage or retrieval system without the prior written permission of the copyright owner, except in the case of brief quotations embodied in critical reviews and certain noncommercial uses permitted by federal copyright law.

This book is presented solely for educational purposes. The author and publisher are not offering legal, financial or professional services advice. While best efforts have been used in preparing this book, the author and publisher make no representations or warranties of any kind and assume no liabilities of any kind with respect to the accuracy or completeness of the contents and specifically disclaim any implied warranties of merchantability or fitness of use for a particular purpose. Neither the author nor the publisher shall be held liable or responsible to any person or entity with respect to any loss or incidental or consequential damages caused, or alleged to have been caused, directly or indirectly, by the information or programs contained herein. No warranty may be created or extended by sales representatives or written sales materials. Every company and/or individual is different and the advice and strategies contained herein may not be suitable for your situation. The services of a competent professional should be utilized.

For information on distribution rights, royalties, derivative works or licensing opportunities on behalf of this content or work, please contact the publisher at the address below, or via email at info@bridgegroup.com.

Bridge Group Communications, LLC
343 Soquel Avenue, #510
Santa Cruz, CA 95062
800-762-4027
www.bridgegroup.com

"The Citizen Leader" is a registered trademark of Bridge Group Communications, LLC.
All rights reserved.

Library of Congress Control Number: 2011912227
ISBN: 978-0-9835683-0-8 (print); ISBN: 978-0-9835683-1-5 (ebook — Kindle);
ISBN: 978-0-9835683-2-2 (ebook — Nook™); ISBN: 978-0-9835683-3-9 (ebook — iBook);
ISBN: 978-0-9835683-4-6 (ebook — Google)

Printed in the United States of America

Edition 1.0: October 2011

Credits
Interior Design by CJ de Heer and 1106 Design
Front and back cover designs by CJ de Heer. Photographs on front cover used with permission of the individuals pictured or by license from iStockphoto®.
Back cover photograph by Chris Schmauch, GoodEye Photography + Design

I dedicate this work to you —

the man, the woman, the young adult or the teenager —

who wants to make a meaningful contribution

at home, at work, in your community and in your world,

and who wants to create a great place for us all to live, work and play.

It's up to you.

Contents

THE CITIZEN LEADER

BE THE PERSON YOU'D WANT TO FOLLOW

We are the ones we are waiting for

There is a river flowing very fast.
It is so swift, there are those who will be afraid.
They will try to hold on to the shore.
They will feel they are being torn apart,
And will suffer greatly.
Know that the river has a destination.
The elders say we must let go of the shore,
Push off into the middle of the river.
And I say, See who is in there with you and celebrate!
At this time in history we are to take nothing personally,
Least of all ourselves.
For, the moment we do, our spiritual growth comes to a halt.
The time of the lone wolf is over.
Gather yourselves together, as we are tonight.
Banish the word "struggle" from your attitude and vocabulary.
All that we do now must be done in a sacred manner
And in celebration.
We are the ones we are waiting for.

> — A prophecy of the Hopi people,
>   a Native tribe from the American Southwest

INTRODUCTION

The Citizen Leader: Be the Person You'd Want to Follow is a guide to help men, women, young adults and teens explore and respond to the questions: *Who am I?* and *How do I want to be in the world?* The book challenges people at all stages of personal and professional life to deepen their commitment to being authentic and courageous so they can say with conviction: *I am a person I'd want to follow.*

The book is structured for you to venture through on your own and at your own pace. It is also designed to let you partner with others — peers, coworkers, family, or friends, in school, at work, at home, in a seminar, in a book club — so together you can use its guidance, exercises and tools to create a forum for reflection, sharing, sharpening, learning and growth.

It is my hope that the insights you derive from *The Citizen Leader* will both enrich your life and help you lead others in efforts to create great places for us all to live, work and play.

The first half of this book dives deeply into *character*, to help readers discern and define who they are today, and who they aspire to be tomorrow and well into the future. The second half provides a tutorial on *citizenship* in which I frame questions and suggest a process of inquiry to prompt and coach readers to ask themselves: *What are the causes that I care about in my community? What initiatives could I champion that would contribute to my community? How can I harness the courage to follow through with the actions that will move the initiative forward?* I call this line of inquiry and application *active citizenship*. It is my belief and experience that a candid assessment of character, a conscious commitment to be the person you'd want to follow and a courageous resolve to be an active citizen are preparation for, and the prerequisites of, engaging leadership — that is, leadership that would inspire other members of a community to want to follow your lead.

This is **not** leadership made quick or easy, **nor** is this leadership dumbed down. There are no such things. Rather, this is leadership learning and lessons drawn from the experience of real people, designed for practical application and intended to benefit anyone with a commitment to being more of a leader — regardless of their title or position, and regardless of the size of their staff, supporters or followers. I draw on two decades of consulting, coaching, teaching graduate students and facilitating leadership seminars in business, government, the military, academia and the not-for-profit world. My audiences have included men, women and young adults, with identities and titles ranging from corporate CEO to entrepreneur to local shop owner, from sales executive to sales associate, from scientist to service industry and social worker, educator to engineer, banker to beautician, construction worker to caregiver, admiral to ensign, lawyer to legislator, Ph.D. to M.B.A. to middle school student, and many more. This guide draws on the wealth and wisdom of their experience, exploration, example, struggle, success, breakdown, breakthrough and sheer determination.

I have written this self-directed guide to be usable by and accessible to everyone. Since most people won't have an opportunity to participate in an organized, company-sponsored or costly seminar on leadership, I have designed this guide to be your de facto workshop. It provides rigorous, thorough, thoughtful (and thought-provoking) leadership guidance and training, with the goal of helping you to grow personally and professionally. For your part, in order to gain the most from the investment of your time and energy as you read through *The Citizen Leader* and work through the exercises, you will need to be both reflective and actively engaged.

My approach to leadership is unique. I identify and then frame your interactions as a leader into six **leadership roles** that you regularly — and sometimes even reluctantly — take on from one moment, meeting or team member to the next.

The *six roles of an active citizen and engaging leader* that I invite you to explore are:

Active Citizen

Visionary and Voice for Tomorrow

Conscience of the Culture

Champion of Innovation and Change

Coach of Your Talent

Trusted Partner and Collaborator

Whichever role you take on, your leadership is only as strong as the *bond* you create with others that allows you to engage *their* enthusiasm to serve, to act and to persevere. Your bond with others, whatever form it assumes — personal, professional, political, academic, spiritual, even virtual — and its capacity to inspire them to action is the *sine qua non* of leadership: its absolutely indispensable and essential thing. Your success as a leader — indeed, the success of those you lead — requires you to take on the right role at the right time. *And,* your success as a leader, and theirs, requires you to express yourself in ways that build and fortify those bonds so that the members of your group will want to follow your lead.

The Citizen Leader, along with its follow-up in the series, *The Citizen Leader in Action,* is designed to give you the practical guidance that will help you build and strengthen those relationships. For each one of these essential roles, my aim is to equip you with a dynamic framework, exercises and diagnostic tools that will help you fortify those bonds in ways that allow you to engage the enthusiasm of your partners and followers to dedicate themselves while delivering on the service and actions that will further your worthy goals. You will emerge a more *active* citizen and *engaging leader* at work, at home and in your communities.

It is my core belief that we are all co-creators of the world in which we live. Our families, schools, places of work, places of worship, neighborhoods and towns — all these are the communities that make up our world. Through our daily behaviors, words, actions and choices, we contribute to the character of these communities, and we shape the world in which we live and work, for ourselves, our families, our friends, our colleagues, our coworkers and our fellow citizens. The prerequisite, as you take on any one of these leadership roles in any one of these communities, is your having a strong sense of *who you are*, first. The foundation for your building strong bonds with and leading others begins with your building a strong bond with and leading yourself. That is the essence of this book and its focus. *The Citizen Leader* is devoted to diving down to the deep truths about yourself that respond to this challenge: "Who are you, that *you* or anyone else would want to follow?"

With real-life stories, illustrations and a fair amount of prompting derived from my 20 years of experience as a consultant, lecturer, teacher and learner, I will pose powerful questions to help you delve into the content of your character. I follow these with an inquiry into the strength of your commitment to contribute to your world in meaningful ways. Character and contributing to one's community are the qualities of an *active citizen* — the first and foundational role for anyone who hopes to reach out and ask anyone else to follow their lead.

Chapters 1–4: Character

Your character is the topic — and the challenge — of the first half of this book.

I begin in Chapter 1 with a call for your curiosity and candor as I ask you to take stock of the qualities you possess as a citizen and as a leader. I also ask you to be forthright about the qualities you hope to strengthen as you set out on this exploration of character and active citizenship. This chapter is an exercise in self-awareness. It is your point of departure and sets the tone for the caliber of reflection, inquiry and honesty that will serve you well and enrich your experience as you journey through the rest of the book.

I follow in Chapter 2 by asking you to clearly identify your candid beliefs about the communities that make up your world — more of a challenge than you might think, at first blush. Character does not live in a vacuum, and so this first line of inquiry fleshes out where your character shows up, and perhaps why it reveals itself the way it does.

In Chapters 3 and 4, I ask you to conduct a rigorous, thorough examination of your values and guiding principles. I will challenge you to substantiate what might start out as a broad bundle of qualities, and then I will guide you through a process that will help you clarify and define the handful of principles that truly reflects *who you are*, today. *And* I will help you articulate and explain who and how you aspire to be in the future, and why. Your character consists of your values and guiding principles. They are your signature. They express who you are to the world. They are the substance you have with which to build and strengthen your relationships with others, or to weaken and break them. I will provide you, here, with focused exercises to help you develop and maintain a quality of character that will inspire others to willingly follow your lead and want to participate, serve, act and persevere as you pursue your worthy goals. These exercises will also help you forge a strength of character that can, and will, hold steady in challenging times and circumstances.

We live among circumstances that test our character every day. We live in an era that barrages us from all sides and online by forces — whether psychological, physical, spiritual or other — that can leave us struggling to know: *What is the right thing to do? How is the right way to be? To act? What is the right thing to say?* Pressure from peers, parents, partners, teachers, bosses; professional pressure, social pressure, popular culture and social media; prospects for personal gain, power, profit, prestige and position; noxious preachers and pundits, prejudice and fear mongering — how can these not fog up our minds, not sicken our hearts? I believe these forces are particularly treacherous for those of you who have not yet developed a personally meaningful set of guiding principles and who are struggling to hang on to a clear, steady sense of who you are in the face of a daily assault by these forces. You deserve better. I have written *The Citizen Leader* to help you get what you richly deserve.

I want this book to help you clear your head, heal your heart. To be sure, by the time we reach our twenties, many of us have given some thought to the values that we would trust to guide our lives. We've had some conversations about them at home, in church or in school, on our team or perhaps in our troop. For me, the encounters took the form of assignments or discussions in social studies classes as well as company orientation programs. They were surely well intended, and the teachers and trainers were sincere in their efforts, but, by and large, they were just dips into the topic — brief, shallow, short-lived. They rarely resulted in the kind of understanding and profound meaning surrounding values that I have since come to cherish. It was not until my early thirties that I truly learned the importance of living strictly and deliberately by principles of my own choosing. It was only *after* I had brought on serious injury to my character (by following someone else's lead to make less-than-honorable choices) that I finally understood: *I am the final arbiter of my actions.*

In the intervening years, I have studied many memoirs, read numerous stories and amassed a large library of self-help workbooks to weave through exercises that aim to have me identify and define my values. As good as many of these books and workbooks have been, most of them did not go far enough to create lasting value. With the exception of a handful of authors (to whom I am enduringly grateful), too many stopped short of taking me on a full journey — from the head to the heart and on through the process of holding myself to account. I found that while some authors led me to markers where I could name my principles and clearly define them, only a few carried me further along to where I could feel my values in my heart, dare to share them confidently with those around me and devote myself to them by way of more consistent action.

In these pages, then, I strive to guide you through a full journey. I commit to give you a roadmap to pursue a rigorous, thorough exploration of who you are today, to prompt you to add who you commit to be tomorrow and to help you express it from your heart. *In addition*, I will give you a framework to help you and the people close to you know and hold you to your promises to consistently be the person you say you will be — in thought, word and deed. For your part, this will require your honesty and humility, your curiosity and courage. At the end of the journey, you will emerge more resolute in your commitment to be the person *you'd* want to follow, and far more apt to be the person anyone *else* would want to follow.

Naturally, you will embark on other journeys of self-discovery later in your life, since personal and professional growth is an ongoing process. This guide will surely prove every bit as useful to you as a roadmap for those future journeys.

Chapters 5–8: Active Citizenship

In the second half of *The Citizen Leader*, I turn your attention to what happens next — tomorrow. I ask you first to assess and then to put into action your desire to become an *active citizen*. These four chapters are a practical, repeatable guide to help you don and demonstrate (perhaps even struggle with) this first foundational role of leadership.

In Chapter 5, you will again consider your community — the people among whom you have the greatest opportunity to make an immediate contribution. I will ask you to articulate your deep beliefs about why you would want to make contributions that could benefit other members of your community. Your answers to these first queries, in and of themselves, will provide you with valuable insights into your commitment to your community and, by extension, your capacity to be a leader whom others in that community would wish to follow.

I devote Chapter 6 to your understanding and applying a framework that makes active citizenship both meaningful and tangible. The Know . . . Care . . . Act framework asks you to identify one initiative that you would be willing to champion, and goes on to prompt you to uncover and then embrace why you care about that initiative. It is your feeling deeply about *why you care* that strengthens your capacity to persevere and bolsters your abilities to engage others' help. Finally, I will ask you to make your active citizenship real: first, by giving you an opportunity to develop a broad set of actions — regardless of fear or risk — that you could take to advance your initiative; and, second, by guiding you through a process that helps you discern and settle on the handful that would have a *compelling effect* on moving your initiative forward, were you to ultimately take them.

Understanding both courage and fear — and choosing to act with courage despite the fear — is the substance of Chapter 7. I will ask you to harness the power of your mental resolve and pair it with your deep-felt caring to arrive at a point where you commit to exercise the courage to follow through with the fearful or risky actions that will carry you to your goal. Over the course of the chapter, I establish courage as a verb — a powerful action verb. *And* I help you to get comfortable with stating "*I courage to* . . ." It is my hope that your experience of *actively expressing* your courage, here, will encourage and embolden you when you are confronted with whether (or not) to take impactful action, both as an active citizen *and* as an engaging leader, well into the future.

In the final chapter of *The Citizen Leader*, I focus on how you can fuel the spirits of those who participate, serve, act and persevere alongside you. Specifically, I guide you through a series of reflective queries to elicit an experience of heartfelt gratitude for someone who has made a meaningful contribution in your community. I prompt you to express that, in turn, in a way that will be heartfelt by your intended receiver. This goes deeper than the appreciation that, well-intentioned though it might be, sometimes sounds and feels as if it's coming from the head — because it is. That kind carries neither the pulse nor the power of heartfelt gratitude that, while it originates in the head, travels to the heart before it is expressed in words and deeds. The heart is the source of the fuel that feeds the human spirit and activates good works. When you express your appreciation from a place of the heart, you strengthen your bond with those who are working and struggling along with you. You are letting them know that you care.

Your ability to master the practice of bringing both head and heart into play when you interact with others is the relationship skill that will serve you best as you step into the other essential roles of a leader and strive to engage the enthusiasm of others to follow your lead. I know that *The Citizen Leader* will prepare you well.

The final pages of this self-directed guide present you with an opportunity to reflect on who and what about you might be changed by virtue of your having journeyed through these eight chapters. It is an opportunity for you to meet yourself anew, to reacquaint and to update your sense of who you are today. Finally, it is an opportunity for you to commit to any new qualities of character that, today, will help you become the kind of person you'd want to follow tomorrow.

Each of the eight chapters provides for *learning through doing* — that is, each one encourages you to apply what you are learning to your life, today. *Application* is an essential ingredient for and investment in your growth. To gain the most from *The Citizen Leader*, be rigorous in your *application* of the material, throughout. To support you in your efforts, I have created a set of online worksheets for you to use and reuse as a tool to capture your thoughts and plan your application now and well into the future (read more on page 14).

The principles that you explore and apply throughout this workbook are foundational to all the other roles of a leader. *The Citizen Leader* firmly lays down the building blocks upon which to develop your capacity to be an *engaging leader*. Yet, if you go no further than you've gone here, yours has *already* been a hero's journey — one made complete both by your commitment to be of such character that you'd want to follow your own lead, and by your courage to put into practice your role as an *active citizen* in your communities.

The original manuscript for this book also covered the five essential roles of an engaging leader. But, according to my initial and intrepid readers (to whom I am very grateful), it seemed overwhelming. I took that feedback as good data and divided the manuscript into two.

In a follow-up series of tutorials, *The Citizen Leader in Action*, I will make each of the remaining leadership roles understandable, personally meaningful and actionable. For each leadership role, I am writing a self-directed guide for you to work through, whether on your own, with a partner or in a small group. These are **not** textbooks of theory. Instead, the form and flow will be more that of practical and practicable field guides in which I will teach you how to apply interactive frameworks that can help you strengthen your bonds with the people you lead as you step into the five roles of an engaging leader. Such roles will require you to: create and communicate a meaningful vision, craft a purposeful culture, lead innovation and change, coach the talented members of your team, build trusting partnership and collaborate broadly. Additionally, in these guides-to-come, I will provide you with practical tools customized for each leadership role; they will help you diagnose, plan, communicate, share decision-making and distribute ownership with others in your group and in your community.

I applaud you for your commitment to learn and grow, personally and professionally — to be an active citizen and to become an engaging leader. It is my hope that the insights you derive from *The Citizen Leader* and *The Citizen Leader in Action* will enrich your life and help you engage the enthusiasm of your partners, your followers and your fellow citizens as you make meaningful contributions at work, at home and in your world — as you create great places for us all to work, to live and to play.

Six Roles of an Active Citizen and Engaging Leader

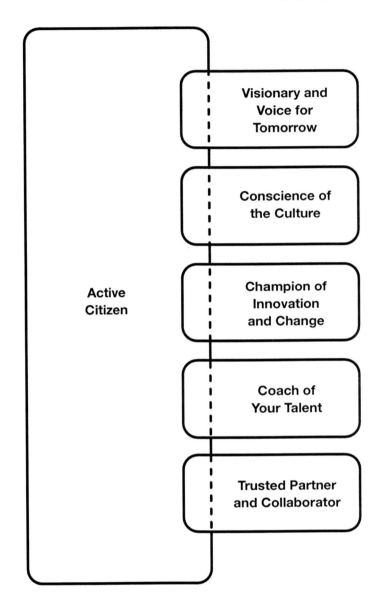

Active Citizen

- Visionary and Voice for Tomorrow
- Conscience of the Culture
- Champion of Innovation and Change
- Coach of Your Talent
- Trusted Partner and Collaborator

*Leadership, at its core, is the **bond** we create with others that engages their enthusiasm to serve, to act and to persevere as we pursue our worthy goals."*

— Peter Alduino, Author, *The Citizen Leader*

How to Use *The Citizen Leader* as a Self-Directed Guide for Personal and Professional Development

I have endeavored to make *The Citizen Leader* accessible to and usable by everyone. There's no doubt that working through the chapters will be hard work — but then again, leadership is hard work. *And* it is rewarding work, for both you and the people you lead.

Here are my thoughts on how you can most benefit as you guide yourself through this exploration of your character as an *active citizen*:

- Approach the questions on each page with an intention to be curious about the truth and candid in your responses.
- Go slowly and deliberately. The progression of questions for each topic is designed to gradually flesh out particular concepts or ideas.
- Be patient. Be thorough. Be expansive in your thinking and responses.
- Linger with your answers. Go deep. Go deeper.
- Be eager to learn about yourself along the way — perhaps meet yourself anew.
- Look for the insights. And ask, "How can I turn my insights into meaningful actions and interactions with others, so that I can strengthen my bonds with them?"
- Apply what you learn. Given all my experience, and with plenty of corroborating evidence to back me up, I am convinced that for your learning to have longevity (or "legs") it must be accompanied by immediate, meaningful, practical

application *and* by equally meaningful and practical application over time. To that end, you will find two resources to help you apply . . . apply . . . apply:

1. Recommendations for *Your Next Steps*

   At the conclusion of both Parts One and Two of the book, you will find a full page of suggested next steps. These will remind you of what you can do over and over again to extend your learning, deepen your growth and strengthen your bonds with others as you continue to make meaningful contributions in your world.

2. Review of Questions

   All the essential questions for each chapter are compiled and presented in the final pages of *The Citizen Leader*. Use this sequential review of questions both to continue to challenge your understanding of and relationship with your values and guiding principles, and to continue to help you apply the frameworks and tools as you participate, serve and lead in your communities.

Capture Your Responses with Online PDF Worksheets

Immediately following each question throughout *The Citizen Leader*, you will find lined spaces to write your responses, and you will find a marker in the upper right-hand corner that refers you to the page of a set of online worksheets containing the same question. (See an example of the lined spaces and marker below.) The online worksheets, formatted as a fill-in PDF document, are available for you to capture your thoughts and responses, and to print, use and store for your own ongoing personal and professional growth and development. These worksheets will make it easier for you to repeatedly draw on the exercises in this book as you apply them to serve your communities well into the future.

See PDF Worksheet p. XX

You may access the full set of fill-in PDF worksheets at:

www.thecitizenleader.com/worksheets-tcl-1

Enhance Your Learning and Growth by Partnering Up

To promote your learning and growth, peer up. Partner with someone who also has a desire to grow as a citizen and as a leader. Or put together a small group of peers. Work together. Remember, "It takes two knives to keep one sharp." If you choose to partner with someone:

- Challenge one another to be thoughtful, to be rigorous, to be fearless.
- Act as a sounding board for one another. Suspend judgment.
- Allow one another to try on and try out ideas, approaches, words and interactions.
- Give one another feedback, and know that only *you* will be — and must be — the final arbiter of your choices and actions. That is an act of leadership.
- Finally, be accountable to yourself and to your partner(s) for answering and following through on the question, "How will I use what I am learning to build my bonds with others in order to engage *their* enthusiasm to participate, serve, act and persevere?"

A Note to Teachers, Trainers and Facilitators

The content of *The Citizen Leader* is comprehensive. There are no ancillary explanatory notes. Nor is there a separate facilitator guide, or the need for one. It's all right here for you, your students and your participants to use in a class, workshop or seminar — objectives, explanations, exercises, learning points, illustrations, real-life stories, next steps and review of questions. The design and the flow enable you to move through the material as if you were using a seminar workbook. Your opportunity and challenge is to develop your own creative presentation.

Finally, I know that teachers and facilitators are constrained in what they can teach by the time available to them and their groups. Know that on the many occasions that I have conducted *The Citizen Leader* as a seminar or workshop, I have found that with focus, guidance and energy, a group can derive meaningful and applicable benefits by investing approximately eight hours of their time and attention working through the chapters.

The Citizen Leader

PART ONE

CHARACTER

CHAPTER

1

Self-Awareness

Your World and You

The chapters that you are about to embark on invite you to explore the deep truths about the qualities of your character, and reveal the strength of your commitment to play an *active* role as a *citizen*, at home, at work and in your communities.

Citizens are the essence of community — any community. Whatever the scope — home, work, school, neighborhood, town, troop, church, temple, support group, sports team — your active participation in efforts to better that community and improve life for everyone is a true act of citizenship.

The questions in these chapters are powerful tools that ask of you deep introspection and reflection. They require your curiosity and humility. And they call on you to be brutally honest *with* yourself and *about* yourself. No judgment is attached to your answers. What is important is that you be rigorous, seek honesty and *own your truth* about who you are at this point in time, as well as who you strive to be.

Your willingness to engage courageously in this journey of questions will help you know the substance and feel the strength of your convictions, your credibility and your courage to lead. Your responses will provide insight into the authentic content of your character and bolster your enthusiasm to engage in your community as an active citizen. *And* they will serve as the foundation for your capacity to rally and guide others to serve and act, make meaningful contributions and help you all create great places to live, work and play.

Your truth will reveal whether you are leading a life of personal integrity — *whether you are a person you or anyone else would want to follow.*

Your truth allows you to decide on your priorities for change, and to commit to fine-tune, adjust or reshape the ways you show up in the world so that your words and actions *are* entirely consistent with who you strive to be as a human being, as a citizen and as a leader.

And finally, your truth will reveal whether and why you care to actively participate in efforts that better your life and the lives of those around you.

It is my belief and experience that with your candid assessment of character, your conscious commitment to be the person you'd want to follow and your courageous resolve to be an active citizen, you will emerge with a strong and steady sense of who you are, and who you commit to be. *And* you will emerge more steadfastly a person others will enthusiastically want to follow.

Let's start by asking the question, "*What is your own truth as a citizen and as a leader, today?*"

On the next few pages, you will find a series of queries to help you mine the answer. I'll be asking: *What do you think your strengths are as a citizen? As a leader? What are the areas that you need to work on? Why?* These are the questions that will help you get started and build your self-awareness. Your responses will serve as a good base camp from which to launch the exploration of your self and your character.

To make the efforts you are about to invest in *The Citizen Leader* meaningful and of lasting value, spend a few hours over the next several days working through these initial exercises before you dig into the rest of the book.

Please know that your warming up with these exercises will enrich your experience as you work through this book and will enhance both your learning and your personal and professional development as a citizen leader.

Exercise: What Does *Citizen* Mean in Your World?

To set the stage, take a few minutes to reflect on the notion of *citizen*. No need to write anything down, but do seriously consider how you would answer these two questions before you move on.

What does *citizen* mean to *you*?
and
How would you define *citizen*?

Now, let's get more specific, and this time jot down your thoughts.

What are the essential qualities, values or behaviors *you* look for in a citizen?

See PDF Worksheet p. 6

Why do you look for *these* qualities in particular?

See PDF Worksheet p. 6

Given what you have written, along with a candid look at your own life:

What strengths do *you* bring to being a citizen?

See PDF Worksheet p. 7

What qualities, values or behaviors do you need or want to *strengthen* as a citizen?

See PDF Worksheet p. 7

Why?

See PDF Worksheet p. 8

My responsibility, our responsibility as lucky Americans, is to try to give back to this country as much as it has given us, as we continue our American journey together."

— Colin Powell, former Secretary of State and former Chairman
   of the Joint Chiefs of Staff

Exercise: What Does *Leader* Mean in Your World?

Now, let's move on to the notion of *leader*. And this time, we'll take a different approach. Instead of answering the questions yourself, ask the people around you for *their* thoughts on what being a leader means to *them*.

Let a few of your colleagues, students, family, friends or acquaintances know that you are exploring the nature of leadership. Ask each one to share a story with you in which they describe a leader whom they look up to — current or past. When they have finished, ask them these next couple of questions and jot down their responses.

What are the essential qualities, values or behaviors *they* look for in a leader?

See PDF Worksheet p. 9

Why are these qualities, values or behaviors important to them?

See PDF Worksheet p. 9

Given what you heard, and being candid as you take a look at yourself:

What strengths do *you* bring to being a leader?

See PDF Worksheet p. 10

The Citizen Leader: Be the Person You'd Want to Follow

What qualities, values or behaviors do you need or want to *strengthen* as a leader?

See PDF Worksheet p. 10

Why?

See PDF Worksheet p. 11

These two series of queries focusing on the notions of *citizen* and *leader* are your starting point. If your purpose for investing your time and energy in *The Citizen Leader* is to become more the person you'd want to follow, and to become more the person that those around you would want to follow, then here you have a preliminary assessment of your strengths and the areas you can work on as you venture further into the book. But know this: in gathering this information (or data, as I like to call it) you are already practicing two of the essential qualities of a great leader — not just a good, but a great leader! Those qualities are curiosity and humility.[1] You'll read and rely more on them in the ensuing chapters. As you continue to draw on these qualities throughout your exploration here, you truly will know yourself better and equip yourself to become and be the person you and they would want to follow.

---

1. The conclusion that personal humility is one of the qualities that differentiates a great leader from a good leader is drawn from the research and findings of Jim Collins cited in *Level 5 Leadership*, Harvard Business Review, January–February 2001.

CHAPTER

Convictions

Community

It is a fundamental tenet of *The Citizen Leader* that citizenship challenges us to contribute to the world around us — that we *act* as citizens when we participate in efforts to better our community and improve life for everyone in it.

Let me propose that the caliber of our actions, or indeed even our willingness to take action at all, is directly proportional to our beliefs and feelings about our community. Ralph Waldo Emerson, the American philosopher and advocate of self-reliance and personal initiative, reminds us that *nothing great was ever achieved without enthusiasm.* So as we begin to explore your role as an active citizen in your community, let's start by asking you to consider your beliefs and feelings about the world in which you have the remarkable opportunity to make an immediate difference — about the communities where you live, work, play and pray.

And herein lies the first challenge. What is community? What do we really mean by community? These are questions that I have struggled with, and still do some-times, even today. So, I'll start by sharing some thoughts with you that have helped me to get clearer on the notion of community. Then we can move on to more clearly identify *your* community and more concretely answer questions about your beliefs, your feelings and your enthusiasm to contribute.

Community. It's one of those words we use as an easy and convenient way to label or group people. Sometimes we say *community* to identify the inhabitants of a geographic area (say, the community of Santa Cruz, California, where I live) or political entities (the community of nations). At other times we say *community* to identify individuals by a host of widely different criteria and affiliations: professional (business, high-tech, medical, military), religious (Christian, Jewish, Muslim), racial and ethnic (black, white, Hispanic, Asian), sporting interests (golf, NASCAR) . . . and the list goes on. Just as often, we use *community* in referring to ourselves as a way to self-identify — to think of ourselves as a part of others rather than apart from them (as in "I am part of the gay community" or "the surf community"). At a fundamental level, *community* conveys a sense of belonging.

Almost every morning for the past two years, I have driven or biked to People's Coffee, about two miles from my home in Santa Cruz, for a triple americano. Everyone behind the counter knows my name, greets me, asks me how I am doing and chats. We've gotten to know a little bit about one another over time. The crew: Curtis (Cordon Bleu master chef turned barista/owner — we trade tales of weekend adventures, in the kitchen or dining out), Austin (avid gardener — we regularly update one another on what is growing, ripening or flowering in our gardens), Andrea (graduate student, multilingual — she and I speak French together), Dan (aspiring musician/ singer who just cut his first CD — very Native American beat — gave me a copy and asked me for my candid feedback) and Cody (café mascot, Australian sheep dog, wanders in and out flashing his watery eyes hoping for a handout).

I am part of the wave of regulars who show up at the café day after day. We recognize one another. We sometimes nod or offer a brief hello. Some of us hang out, sip, read, write or do whatever it is we do on our laptops, phones or iPads. People's is a place of familiarity in the morning. We are the morning crowd. But it leads me to ask, is that all we are — the morning *crowd*? — or is our band of regulars a community? Do a group of people who share a common space, frequent the same coffee bar or live in the same dormitory or co-op or even zip code constitute "community"? What does it take to transform crowd into community?

I graduated from Bowdoin College in Brunswick, Maine, some 30 years ago. To this day, I regularly get mailings of its alumni magazine, newsletters from the president, annual requests for donations and a yearly calendar with pictures of the campus. By virtue of my being an alum, I am and will always be connected with Bowdoin, and the college will try to stay connected with me. In fact, we band of alumni are oftentimes referred to as part of the "Bowdoin community." I have deep affections for my college. I do my part by occasionally reading their online daily newspaper and their monthly email bulletins. But is this virtual connection enough for me to honestly say that I feel part of the Bowdoin community?

Is sharing an interest enough to constitute "community"? Interests in common often lead to a self-selected identity that we willingly, even eagerly, assume. Look to the citizens of Red Sox Nation. Is this band of passionate fans a community?

Or can sharing an activity build a community? Hundreds of surfers live in Santa Cruz, many of whom know one another and have been surfing together for years, even decades. Most share the waves. Some, though, band together and can act fiercely possessive of what they consider "their break," a localism that can create friction with outsiders. Mind you, an outsider can just be a surfer from the other side of town. An outsider can also be someone who surfs on a different-length surfboard. So, when I hear or read about the "surf community," I wonder what it means.

The overarching question remains the same: What makes community?

For an answer, I look first to a dictionary. Webster's informs me that *community* derives from the Latin prefix *con*, meaning "together." It *also* comes to us from the Latin *munis*, which means "performing services." Ahh! I begin to see deeper, and perhaps appreciate the overlooked essence of the word: *community* is individuals who *together serve* and support one another.

Now we're getting somewhere. More than identity (Bowdoin graduate, Red Sox fan, surfer), community means involvement: involvement with others with an aim to serve and support one another. Community is active. It is engagement. It is participation. Community is **not** a spectator sport.

That meaning has gusto. Community connotes a group of people in whom I can place my faith and trust to help me out when and if I'm in need, and to whom, by the same token, I'd be willing to lend a hand if one of them were in need. We're all in this together, and our strength is in our unity. Sign me up.

So, let's focus on *your* communities — the various bands or crowds with whom you come together (be they real or virtual) to support and serve one another. Look all around you: at work, at home, in school, at play, in support groups, in faith-based groups, in neighborhood groups, on teams, in troops, in virtual groups and in the many ways and places that you and others come together to serve and support one another. Each of us probably belongs to several communities. Put an identity to these groups of individuals with whom you connect through your active and supportive participation, not begrudgingly but willingly, not because you have to but because you want to.

Who are your communities?

<table>
<tr><td>See PDF Worksheet p. 13</td></tr>
</table>

Focus on just one of the communities of which you are a member. In your mind's eye, picture several of the individuals in that community and write down your response:

Who is in this particular community?

<table>
<tr><td>See PDF Worksheet p. 13</td></tr>
</table>

You identified *this* group of individuals because you all actively participate in supporting or serving one another. As such, allow yourself to rightfully call yourself a citizen of that community.

Citizen is a deeply honorable title. Yes, it is most commonly a designation bestowed by an accident of birth or location. But it can be so much more. In a truer form, citizenship is a merit that we earn by extending ourselves to others and contributing to the world around us. Citizens are involved and engaged. They are participants. They are doers. They are *not* spectators. In essence, we earn the right to call ourselves citizens because we are willing to actively participate in efforts that better a community and improve life for all. In so doing, it is we who, by the virtue and the value of our contribution, transform ourselves from just one among a crowd into an active member of a particular community.

Allow yourself to own and relish your right and your role. Go ahead, say it out loud: "I am an active citizen of _____ community!"

write it here

Convictions

The reflections and questions on the previous few pages had you clarify your thoughts on the notion of community, and focus on the ones in your world. In particular, I asked you to picture the faces of the members of one specific community so that it could be more personal than abstract. With those individuals in mind, now you can focus on your beliefs and feelings about that group and your place in that community. In short, now you can examine your convictions. It is the quality of your internal convictions that will influence your willingness to engage in current and continuing efforts to take the actions that will serve and support the other members of your community and make for meaningful contributions now and into the future.

So, let's take a look at your convictions about the community of which you just proclaimed yourself an active citizen.

Candidly and honestly respond to the following questions:

What are my strong beliefs and feelings about this community?

See PDF Worksheet p. 14

What are the more significant services or work that *I am doing* in this community?

See PDF Worksheet p. 14

I do this service or work because . . .

See PDF Worksheet p. 15

I care about my service or work because . . .

See PDF Worksheet p. 15

I am of the mind that the person who has experience as an active citizen will possess the unique capacity to engage others as a leader.

By the same token, I feel wary of those who wear the mantle of leader, but who, on closer inspection, show little appreciable depth as citizens. I look to see whether an individual has in their history any evidence of service and contribution to their communities, or whether instead theirs is a record of activity undertaken largely for the purposes of self-advancement or enrichment. If the evidence supports the latter, I ask myself whether their conduct as a leader would be any different.

In my experience, self-serving behavior cloaked as leadership is a sham. It is the stuff of those who have traded integrity for expedience, for egocentric satisfaction, for selfishness. But it is not the stuff of engaging leadership, and it is certainly not the stuff of citizenship.

How does my service or work improve life for others?

See PDF Worksheet p. 16

In some circles, leadership has gotten a bad rap because of the people in leadership positions who have given it that.

Right here, right now, we have a chance to change that. During our lives, most of us will face many challenges that will invite us, if not require us, to lead. When we step into the roles of an engaging leader, the content of our character will shape the relationships that we form with the other members of our community. The ways in which we *express* our character will enhance or diminish our capacity to engage their willingness and their enthusiasm *to want to* participate, serve, act and persevere. You have the opportunity to be of such character that your partners will not only follow your lead, but will surge out ahead of you — and will do so because, together, you are striving to make contributions that are meaningful to everyone.

Let's look closely at character and the role it plays in one's being a citizen leader.

3

Credibility

Personal Integrity and Credibility

Character is the embodiment and the expression of our guiding principles and values. It is who we are on the inside, and what we show on the outside. Our guiding principles and values are the promises we make to ourselves about how we will behave, both in private and in the world at large. When we live up to those promises — when we act consistently with what it is we say we stand for, and consistently deliver on our promises (even when no one else is looking) — we are living in **personal integrity**.

For most of us, our personal values don't remain a private affair, either. We often share them with the other members of our community. We make a promise to them, *and* we give them the expectation that we will conduct ourselves in ways that are consistent with our promises. By living up to those promises, we build our believability — and strengthen our **credibility**.

Credibility derives from the Latin verb *credo*, which means *I believe*. Our believability — or our credibility — rests in the eyes of others. Our credibility manifests in others as *I believe you. I believe you because your actions are consistent with your promises.* Our credibility is other people placing their faith and trust in us. It is their having faith that we will continue to behave and speak and act in ways that adhere to the expectations we have created or stated.

Naturally, we all trip up on occasion and do things that are against what we say we stand for. To the degree that we have built a well of credibility in the minds of others, we can ask for forgiveness and be forgiven. But, if the pattern of our actions, behaviors and words over time start to suggest something other than what we claim about ourselves, then it's that pattern that begins to speak the louder.

Now, none of us is perfect, and we may all momentarily step on our principles or hot headedly transgress them. That's the cost that comes along with being human, yet a basically healthy credibility can weather the missteps.

But what about those occasions when we consciously choose to ignore our principles and "*make an exception to the rule*"? Whether for expediency's sake or for our own gain, believing that the ends justify the means can result in giving others reason to pause, wonder or doubt that we are who we claim to be. If our adherence to guiding principles is the bedrock of our credibility, then shedding those values — regardless of the reason — is a blow that can fracture the foundation that others rely on when choosing whether to believe, trust, join or follow us. At its most damaging, *a pattern of making an exception to the rule* gives others cause to say to themselves *non credo — I do not believe.*

Consider the employer, the manager or the team leader who claims to highly value the principle of work–life balance, but who regularly texts or emails queries after hours, over the weekend or during vacation time, *and* expects a timely response. What message is this individual really giving about what she or he is committed to? What happens to their credibility vis-à-vis their professed principle of work–life balance?

The following series of exercises will help you to explore in depth the current state of your personal integrity and credibility by answering two critical questions:

1. *What are the promises I make about how I will conduct myself, both in private and out in the world?*
2. *How consistently do I live up to the promises I make to myself and to others?*

Exercise: Guiding Principles and Values (I)

Let's start by taking a broad-brush approach to the topic. Using the list below, select the ten or so guiding principles and values that resonate with you most. In other words, which of these represent the main promises that you live by, both privately and publicly?

Acceptance   Accomplishment   Accountability   Achievement   Adventure   Affiliation   Approval   Attractiveness   Authenticity   Autonomy   Balance   Beauty   Caring   Challenge   Change   Collaboration   Comfort   Commitment   Common Good   Compassion   Competence   Conformity   Consensus   Contribution   Cooperation   Courage   Courtesy   Creativity   Decisiveness   Dependability   Discipline   Duty   Ecology   Equality   Excellence   Excitement   Exploration   Facts   Fairness   Faith   Fame   Family   Fear   Fitness   Flexibility   Forgiveness   Freedom   Friendship   Fun   Generosity   God's Will   Gratitude   Green   Growth   Harmony   Health   Helpfulness   Home   Honesty   Honor   Humility   Humor   Independence   Industry   Inner Peace   Innovation   Integrity   Intimacy   Justice   Knowledge   Leisure   Loved   Loving   Loyalty   Mastery   Mindfulness   Moderation   Money   Nonconformity   Nurturance   Openness   Order   Partnership   Passion   Peace   Play   Pleasure   Power   Prestige   Productivity   Profit   Realism   Recognition   Respect   Responsibility   Rigor   Risk   Romance   Safety   Security   Self-Acceptance   Self-Control   Self-Esteem   Self-Knowledge   Service   Sexuality   Simplicity   Solitude   Spirituality   Stability   Teamwork   Thrift   Tolerance   Tradition   Transparency   Trust   Wealth   Win   Others . . .

While you should feel free to draw from these concepts, this list is not meant to limit you in any way. It is intended as a starting point to prompt your thinking. If there are other values that apply but are not reflected in this list, please write them down on the next page.

There is no right answer, good answer or bad answer. There is, however, the important answer: It is important that you capture the principles or values that resonate most strongly with you when you consider the ways in which you go about behaving, talking with others and making choices in your day-to-day life.

Use the space below to capture your thoughts. Feel free to cross out, change, erase, rewrite or otherwise alter your responses until you get a list of ten to twenty that feels right to you. Your answers are not carved in stone, and you will have ample opportunity to refine them. This first go-round is but one of many iterations that you will proceed through as you articulate the principles and values that you know or believe to be at the very foundation — at the very core — of who you are, and who you strive to be.

See PDF Worksheet p. 18

Exercise: Guiding Principles and Values (II)

Let's continue to explore.

Take a look at the work you do or the service you regularly perform in your community.

What principles or values does that work or service reflect?

Think back on how you chose to spend your time during the last few weeks.

What principles or values were reflected in the choices you made about how you spent your time?

EXAMPLE

Every now and then, when I've asked my clients to respond to these questions, one of them has challenged me to do the same. So, let me share with you one of those times to illustrate how to approach these last questions. On one particular day several years ago, I was with a group of men and women who worked for an electricity generation company. In attendance was a broad range of individuals, from senior managers to linesmen (the guys who sling transmission cables between poles and towers).

"Okay, Peter, if we're going to open our kimonos, so are you," they said to me. My opting out was not an option.

I let the questions float freely in my mind, and then in a short while jotted down the words and images that seemed to resonate with me and caused me to respond strongly:

- airplane
- hands clasping one another
- feet with wings
- bicycle

What did these say about my guiding principles or values?

Airplane: I had spent many, many hours flying to client locations far afield of my home (at the time, it was in San Francisco) in the prior few weeks. **I was dedicated to my clients**, and traveled widely to conduct leadership workshops for their employees.

Hands clasping: My work during the many hours in the leadership workshops was all about **offering a helping hand** to people.

Feet with wings, and a bicycle: Despite my days on the road, **I put in the hours to stay physically fit**. In the evenings while far from home, I would go running for an hour. When at home on the weekends, I spent most of Saturday riding my bike over and through the hills north of San Francisco.

This was a start in sharing my principles and values with my clients' employees. I would continue to mine the answers to the questions about guiding principles and values as I considered my response to all the questions that follow below.

Now it's your turn. I invite you to respond to the first two questions I started with. And then to consider a few more questions that will help you explore even further.

What principles or values does your work or service reflect?

See PDF Worksheet p. 19

What principles or values were reflected in the choices you made about how you spent your time during the last few weeks?

See PDF Worksheet p. 19

Describe a few of the interactions you had at work and in your personal life over the past few days. What are the key principles or values that your interactions seem to demonstrate?

See PDF Worksheet p. 20

What are some of the routine choices that you have made in the course of the past several days, even those you made when no one else was looking? What words or concepts most accurately capture the principles or values underlying those choices?

See PDF Worksheet p. 20

Now put yourself in the shoes of some of the people with whom you interact at work, at home and in regular daily life. What principles and values do you think *others* would say they *regularly* see play out in the ways you behave, talk with others, make choices and generally interact in your community?

See PDF Worksheet p. 21

The Citizen Leader: Be the Person You'd Want to Follow

Pattern of My Actions

In the prior exercise, you had the opportunity to record your thoughts and ideas about the values and guiding principles that inform your behaviors, words, choices and interactions with the world around you.

This next series of exercises asks you to be brutally honest with yourself about what really *is* accurate — meaning, which principles are supported by the actual *pattern of your actions*, day in and day out. You are not looking for the exception to the rule. Nor are you looking for what you (or others) might expect of yourself. Rather, look for the essential few principles that are supported by your regular, consistent behavior.

So, filter through all the possible candidates, and settle on the essential few for which you have ample evidence to state, "These principles are supported by *the pattern of my actions*."

For instance, if you say that *health* is one of the principles that regularly guide your actions, then look for evidence that supports your claim:

Do you **choose** to exercise regularly? Did your exercise regime last week support the claim? Do you make choices that allow you to eat nutritional and well-balanced meals? Do the groceries you bought last week and the meals you ate out support the claim?

In essence, does the *pattern of your actions* provide enough evidence to support your assertion that *health* is one of the core values that guide your behaviors and your choices? If so, that's good data.

If not, that is not an indication of good or bad. It is simply an honest assessment of what is accurate. That's also good data. This is not to say that you don't *aspire to* embody the value of *health* in your day-to-day actions. It's just that the pattern of your actions at the present time doesn't support it. Perhaps in the future you will commit to regularly behaving and making the day-to-day choices that provide enough evidence to support your saying that health is indeed one of the core principles by which you conduct your life. The beauty of it is, that's a choice you will always have.

So, if the first few exercises had you thinking off the top of your head, this next set of exercises will begin to have you look at your behavior in a variety of contexts. In these contexts, you can examine the evidence and data that show you which of the ten or so values you picked come into play most often. This will allow you to begin to narrow down this larger list to the *handful* that lie at the core of your being — the core of your character.

I use the word *handful* deliberately, for, despite the number of values or principles that you might have noted on the preceding few pages, my experience doing this process with thousands of people has convinced me that there really are only a handful that permeate our day-to-day actions. And since intelligent people can debate about the number that constitutes a handful, let's just say the range is between four and seven core values. It is this handful that captures the accurate character of who you are and how you are perceived.

The other reason for this next step is that it will help you to find those values and principles that are truly real and honest. Most other exercises of this nature that I have come across ask people simply to pick what they *believe* to be their values, but rarely go further to the point of asking them to find the data in their daily lives that confirms their beliefs. To my mind, this does a tremendous disservice to the individual, to their integrity and credibility. As a colleague has often reminded me, "We are all entitled to our own opinions, but we are not entitled to make up our own data." So, as an alternative to the risk of being blinded (if not weakened) by our unconfirmed or unverified opinions of ourselves, we can be truer to ourselves (and to others) by rigorously and thoroughly seeking to discern our actual values — by looking at our behaviors, by scrutinizing the *data*. With my clients, I am always encouraging them to gather data.

For example, one of my consulting clients, the CEO of a multi-billion-dollar consumer products company, regularly expressed his desire and openness to hearing diverse points of view at his staff meetings, He routinely asked his senior staff to include more junior members of their departments in the discussions, so they could gain experience from what he hoped would be a lively airing of ideas. Privately, to me, he expressed his frustration that often he felt there was not a good, robust exchange of ideas. My response, on more than one occasion, was, "That's good data." In other words, he prided himself on being someone who valued open communication, but the data suggested that his staff, and especially the junior staff, experienced him differently. By putting aside the opinion he had of himself, and instead honestly looking at the data, he could discern a more accurate picture of who he was in the eyes of others. This, then, would be his point of departure for reflecting on what he might be doing to contribute to the situation — to their reluctance to engage more rigorously in discussions. Equipped with this data, he could then ask himself what he could do differently.

Just remember, the point here is to be honest with yourself, not to judge yourself for the answers. The more honest you are, the more personal integrity you will experience, and the more credibility you will have with others.

Exercise: Guiding Principles and Values (III)

To begin this process, let's get a better handle on the values you have already selected by taking a deeper look at how you would describe each of the ten or so principles you identified. For example, let's go back to the value of *health*. If, in fact, you do say that *health* is one of the values that regularly guides your behaviors, words and choices, then describe what *health* really means. Describe with as much clarity and in as much detail as you can draw from your day-to-day experience what your value of *health* looks like by way of your actual behaviors, words and choices. The depth of your principles is in the details that you provide.

Here are two examples from my own life. The first I draw from my own handful of personal values. The second is a principle that was shared with me by a client during one of our executive coaching sessions.

Value: *Honesty*

What this value looks like day to day by way of my actual behaviors, words and choices:

1. *I strive to offer my true thoughts and opinions, to represent the facts accurately and to speak and act truthfully and honestly with myself and with others.*
2. *I keep my word and promises, to myself and to others.*

Value: *Diversity*

What this value looks like day to day by way of my actual behaviors, words and choices:

1. *I include individuals with diverse experiences and knowledge on my projects.*
2. *I actively seek out differing points of view before making important choices.*
3. *I insist on and support the members of my group doing the same.*

In the space that follows, please break down each one of *your* values into the specific ways they manifest in your life. What do they look like day to day? What behaviors, words and choices comprise the value?

A Value:

> See PDF Worksheet p. 22

What this value looks like day to day by way of my actual behaviors, words and choices:

> See PDF Worksheet p. 22

B Value:

> See PDF Worksheet p. 22

What this value looks like day to day by way of my actual behaviors, words and choices:

> See PDF Worksheet p. 22

C Value:

See PDF Worksheet p. 23

What this value looks like day to day by way of my actual behaviors, words and choices:

See PDF Worksheet p. 23

D Value:

See PDF Worksheet p. 23

What this value looks like day to day by way of my actual behaviors, words and choices:

See PDF Worksheet p. 23

E Value:

See PDF Worksheet p. 24

What this value looks like day to day by way of my actual behaviors, words and choices:

See PDF Worksheet p. 24

F Value:

See PDF Worksheet p. 24

What this value looks like day to day by way of my actual behaviors, words and choices:

See PDF Worksheet p. 24

(G) Value:

See PDF Worksheet p. 25

What this value looks like day to day by way of my actual behaviors, words and choices:

See PDF Worksheet p. 25

(H) Value:

See PDF Worksheet p. 25

What this value looks like day to day by way of my actual behaviors, words and choices:

See PDF Worksheet p. 25

(I) Value:

See PDF Worksheet p. 26

What this value looks like day to day by way of my actual behaviors, words and choices:

See PDF Worksheet p. 26

(J) Value:

See PDF Worksheet p. 26

What this value looks like day to day by way of my actual behaviors, words and choices:

See PDF Worksheet p. 26

Exercise: Guiding Principles Dashboard — Self-Assessment

Now that you have described what each of the values looks like in your day-to-day life, let's examine the data — *your* data — from a slightly different angle. Using the following self-assessment grid, write down your guiding principles and values in the first column.

See PDF Worksheet p. 27

For the next week, pay close attention to your interactions with others at work, at home and in your community. Keep a log and make note of the times you either demonstrate or deviate from your values. Be honest with yourself — that is, give yourself credit for the times your behaviors, words and choices do demonstrate the guiding principles you have written down. *And* be candid with yourself about the times when they *do not*.

At the end of the week ask yourself: *"To what degree have my behaviors, words and choices regularly demonstrated the principles that I have written down?"* The key is *regularly*.

Score yourself. Using values from 1 to 5, give yourself an overall score for the frequency that you believe your behaviors, words and choices *regularly demonstrated* each of your guiding principles over the week.

	Seldom	Sometimes	About Half the Time	Often	Almost Always
	①	②	③	④	⑤

My Guiding Principles and Values	Behaviors	Words	Choices
EXAMPLE Value: *Diversity*	4	5	3
Ⓐ Value:			
Ⓑ Value:			
Ⓒ Value:			
Ⓓ Value:			
Ⓔ Value:			
Ⓕ Value:			
Ⓖ Value:			
Ⓗ Value:			
Ⓘ Value:			
Ⓙ Value:			

For each item that you scored below 4 on the dashboard, ask yourself:

1. Why did I not give a score of 4 to 5?
2. What would I need to be doing differently to raise the score to a 4 or a 5?

EXAMPLE

Value: *Diversity*

1. *While I talk of actively seeking out differing points of view, I am not often proactive in soliciting other people's ideas. I typically get so attached to my own way of doing things that I do not want others to interfere.*
2. *I need to accept and trust that other members of my group (and the members of my family, for that matter) have valuable insights to contribute, and I need to make the effort to regularly ask for and bounce around their ideas.*

Your turn:

See PDF Worksheet p. 28

See PDF Worksheet p. 28

Paper Cuts

Part One: The Sting

I try to lead my life in accordance with a handful of guiding principles that I promise myself to make *nonnegotiable*. I feel that these promises are the person I want to be, the person I would be proud to be. I feel that if I can keep these promises to myself and to others, then I will be living in integrity — I will have nothing for which to reproach myself. These are my handful, and what they mean to me:

Dare to be true: Speak and act truthfully with myself and others, and encourage others to do the same.

Honor others: Treat everyone with dignity and respect (this goes for animals and nature, too).

Health: Make choices that are healthy for the mind, body and spirit.

Do good work in service of the common good: Make sure my work is of high caliber and that it is about making a contribution to the world around me.

Be fair: Choose the path of fairness in all my dealings.

Connection: Invest face-time or phone-time (as opposed to text or online) to connect with family and friends.

By and large, I live up to my promises. But every now and again, I trip up — I fall out of integrity. The curious thing is that sometimes I see it coming, or, more precisely, I *feel* it coming. I know when I am on the edge, about to fall, because in that moment, something inside of me stings. It's an instantaneous searing hurt, like when I get a paper cut. And, it gets my full and undivided attention. In that moment, I know that I have a choice to come back to integrity.

Let me give you an example. A few months ago, I went into an Apple store. I was going in to buy a battery for my laptop, a carrying case for my iPod and a new power cord. Just as I was approaching the register, the sales associate who was helping me offered: "We have a 5 percent 'education' discount. Are you an educator?" I hesitated, and I said, "Well, no . . . well, yes." I said, "Listen, I'm in private business, but my business is education." And he asked, "Well, do you teach at a university?" I responded, again with hesitation, "Yeah." And he finished with, "Can I see your university ID?" I had an ID card from the University of California, Berkeley where I had served as a visiting member of the faculty. That had been two years earlier.

I was no longer teaching there. But there was no expiration date on the card.

I felt the sting.

What was I thinking?

"Hey, I'm always keen to save a few dollars?"

"Hey, he offered, and he'll never know the difference?"

I honestly don't know. But I do know that, in that moment, an awareness flashed through my mind that if I kept going on this trajectory — if I *knowingly misrepresented* the truth (even if the sales associate would not have known the difference) — I would be violating my nonnegotiable: *Dare to be true*. Something, somewhere inside of me stung — a sting that commanded my attention.

What I need and want to do in moments like this is pay heed. When it stings, I need and want to pause, and ask: "What am I doing here to generate this hurt?" *and* "What do I need to do right here and right now so that I do not make it worse?" Absent that presence of mind to heed my conscience flashing *WARNING, WARNING*, I risk aggravating the hurt — falling further out of integrity with myself.

If I ignore the warning, and fall out of integrity, I just might "get away with it."

But what about the next time when I am flirting with violating *dare to be true*. Will I think twice?

How about the time after that, when I might stand to gain by making *an exception to the rule* if I set aside my principles?

How about the time after that, when I don't think twice because in the grand scheme of things I rationalize, "It's no big deal. It won't amount to anything"?

How about the time after *that*, when I am found out, and I fracture my credibility?

If I ignore the warning, and fall out of integrity with myself, it can and it *does* amount to something. In the grand scheme of things, each time I knowingly repeat this small kind of cheating — each time I set aside *dare to be true* — I put my character at risk.

With repeated injury, sooner or later I risk fundamental change. Sooner or later, I risk growing numb to the sting. I anesthetize my conscience. But what's worse, what's sad, is that I lose the ability to feel or connect with the liveliness that *dare to be true* once contributed to my life and the lives of the people around me. I am fundamentally changed because part of me, part of my *self*, dies.

And what appears in its place is a redefined self, a redefined character — a character that is known by a new pattern of behaviors, words and actions. Where *dare to be true* once guided my life and contributed to the shape of my world, now *knowingly misrepresent* guides my conduct. I haven't really gotten away with anything. Each transgression stays with me in my repository of life experiences. With repeated practice, I perfect a new persona. And, where *dare to be true* used to be who I was, now *knowingly misrepresent* is who I am.

Sting: It helps me safeguard the only thing I can truly call my own.

I am human. Sometimes I ignore the warning. I screw up. As human beings, we are all prone to behaving and speaking in ways that go against our grain. And sometimes, perhaps more often than not, it is in the smallest ways. At times I screw up when I'm impatient, or I'm angry, or I'm feeling entitled, or lazy or tired. And when I do fall out of integrity — when I do act in violation of one of my closely held values — I try to make amends. I try to set the record straight.

But, much more often than not, I strive to be deliberate about my behaviors, my words and my actions. I strive to be deliberate that they reflect who I am and who I want to be. And **when it stings, I pay heed**.

On the whole, I have come to think that *sting* is a really good thing.

But in that moment (at the Apple store) . . .

. . . I showed the sales associate the expired faculty ID. I got away with bending the truth. No, I got away with *knowingly misrepresenting* the truth. My ID card allowed me $5 off on one purchase and $8 off on another. Total was a $13 discount on a purchase of $260. I left the store feeling the sting. I felt the sting for intentionally and knowingly lying for the sake of $13.

I am able to relate all these events and thoughts so vividly because I recorded them on my iPod literally five minutes after this happened while sitting in my car. Now, as I re-listen to my voice, I can hear myself shouting, "For $13, what were you thinking!" for having willfully violated my guiding principle *dare to be true*.

So, I tried to regroup. I got out of my car, went back into the store, back to the sales associate, and said that while I *had been* a lecturer, I was not currently employed by UC Berkley.

His response: "No worries, it's already in the system!"

For him it was no worries. For me, on the other hand, I was furious. At myself!

Part Two: Paying Heed

Paying heed to a sting that violates your core is an act of love: love for yourself.

There are as many ways of going about life as there are human beings on the planet. But I fundamentally believe that there is only one way of going about our life, and that is to go about *our* life by being true to our *self* — true to whatever or however we commit our *self* to be. When I am paying heed, I am being true to myself. When I pay heed, I am loving and caring enough about my *self* to hold myself accountable to the promises that *I* make to myself.

When my behaviors or words or actions betray my stated principles, that's reason enough to give me pause, and make me ask what I truly stand for. If others observe that I am repeatedly unwilling or unable to hold myself to the standards of my values, it is probably reason enough to give them pause, too. More damaging, it is likely reason enough to make them question my trustworthiness and integrity. And it gets worse. It could well be enough to cause them to ask whether their betraying their *own* principles is what *they* might also need to do, in order to gain or get ahead or stay ahead.

They is not an abstract term. *They* consist of the men and women *and* children who inhabit our world. *They* are our families, our friends, our colleagues, our coworkers. *They* are the members of our communities.

Paying heed, then, is an act of love both for ourselves *and* for the people we love.

In the times when we do go against our grain, it's important to learn from it. It's important to have the humility to ask ourselves, "What just happened, and why?" We can grow stronger in our resolve and our commitment to adhere to our principles, and to model a way of being and living that we would want to share with the people we love, that we would want our own children to embrace and defend.

This is how each one of us creates a stronger world, a more principled and a more purposeful world. This is how each one of us creates the kind of world we want to work in and live in. This is how we teach our children or the generation that comes after us the deeper meaning of love, for themselves and for others.

Curiosity and Humility: Prerequisites to Personal Growth and Mastery

In my introduction to the chapter, I said that this exploration of your deep truths and commitment to be an active citizen and engaging leader would demand your powers of introspection, reflection and curiosity. I asked you to draw on these personal powers to discern and define the guiding principles at the core of your being — at the core of your character.

On the previous pages, you gathered **data** about your guiding principles by reflecting on your beliefs about yourself, and by observing your actual behaviors in the past few weeks. That data, when closely examined, informed you more accurately of the pattern of your actions. It is entirely possible that, despite what you might have initially believed, your observations and the resulting **information** allowed you to learn a bit more about yourself — and to identify the *handful* of principles that reside at your core. Good, bad or indifferent, that **knowledge** is essential if you are to **understand** your behaviors and actions *and* to **understand** how and why the people around you interact with you and react to you the way they do.

Perhaps this illustration will help you visualize the journey you are taking. The driving force along the way is your curiosity. As such, it stands to reason that if you allow your curiosity to weaken or wane at any point, so too will your progress toward a fuller understanding of yourself.

Curiosity *n* : the desire to investigate and learn

I ask you to keep up your momentum.

As a next step of your growth in self-awareness, I invite you — even challenge you — to find out what the people around you would say are the values or guiding principles that characterize the pattern of your actions. And the best way to find out is to simply ask them: an inquiry that will demand your continuing curiosity, and perhaps some courage.

On the following pages, you have a *Guiding Principles Dashboard* designed to help you collect feedback from others. This version enables you to gather quantitative data from people around you about *their* perception of whether or with what frequency you demonstrate the principles you write down. Additionally, this dashboard lets you ask them for feedback about what you might do differently, by way of your actions, to adhere to those principles more regularly. This data can help you strengthen your credibility in their eyes.

Make no mistake about it, this part is an exercise in humility. Humility derives from the Latin *humus*, meaning earth, and the Greek for *on the ground*. Humility, then, is a state of coming down to earth, of getting grounded in our humanity — of loosening ego in favor of finding out the truth about ourselves. Humility is the great liberator: It liberates us from the bondage of our own self-image, and it liberates others to care about us by helping us become more self-aware.

At this moment of inquiry, try to suspend judgment about what you believe about yourself, or about what others are saying. Instead, listen, learn, seek to fully understand and be grateful for the courage and care that others are showing by agreeing to give you their feedback. To truly find out about yourself, combine your humility with your curiosity, both when you give yourself feedback *and* when you ask for it from others.

Mind you, this is not for the weak of heart, as the following story illustrates.

Consider two managers who asked me to conduct leadership workshops for their employees, but who did *not* initially intend to participate in the sessions, suggesting they did not need to go through it themselves. One was the director of a marketing group for a large consumer products company, the other a Vice President for Training and Development in the financial services industry. To both managers, I suggested that they might be well served to engage along with their staffs, so that at the very least they could familiarize themselves with the material and be able to coach individuals on an ongoing basis. They ultimately agreed to attend.

Both managers received feedback (anonymous) that was considerably less favorable than they had anticipated. The marketing manager expressed her disappointment at the feedback, and excused it by saying that the people who filled out the forms probably got confused about the scoring system (never mind that these people's jobs were to regularly design, conduct and interpret surveys to gather data!). The Vice President for Training and Development said nothing to me, but I later learned that he individually met with each one of his team members and told them why the scores were "wrong."

You should know that during both workshops, members of their teams privately confided in me that their managers were "the problem."

Now, in fairness, no one can be all things to all people. That is not the goal. The important objective in asking for feedback is to consider the data, and ask yourself, candidly, "What is the message here, and how can I take advantage of it to fine-tune or grow?" Curiosity and humility are necessary elements at play, all along the way.

The CEO of the multi-billion-dollar consumer products company whom you met earlier in this chapter had the curiosity and humility to ask for feedback so that he could understand why, during his staff meetings, he was not getting a good, robust exchange of ideas. He found out that, by and large, his staff did not feel that he was willing or open to listening to diverse points of view, despite his professed desire.

Instead of dismissing the feedback as confused or wrong, he simply asked some of the individuals who had given him the feedback, "Why do you say that?" and "What could I be doing differently?" That's curiosity and humility at play. And then he listened.

There was neither pushback nor "Yes, but . . ." Instead, he showed patience and a desire to take it all in and strive to understand. With all the data, he could reflect, and then decide on what he needed do differently, or more frequently, to generate the lively airing of ideas that he felt was necessary for him to make clear, informed choices for the business.

Tool: Guiding Principles Dashboard — Feedback from Others

Now it's your turn. Let me offer some guidelines for how to go about using this tool and asking others for feedback.

1. Write your name at the top of each page.

2. Write down your guiding principles and values *and their day-to-day meaning* in the first column of the grid. By writing the day-to-day meaning, you let others know how you define the value, and allow them to give you more informed feedback.

   You might find it convenient to use a stand-alone PDF version of this dashboard that you can fill in and give or send to others. It is available online for you to fill in and download at **www.thecitizenleader.com/worksheets-tcl-1**.

3. Ask yourself:
   - *Who are seven to ten people with whom I interact closely — at work, among friends and at home?*
   - *Who among them (five to seven people) would be willing to give me an honest, objective assessment of the pattern of my actions?*

   Jot down their names:

   > See PDF Worksheet p. 29

4. Talk to each person individually. Let them know that you are exploring the nature of credibility, and would like to invite them to give you candid feedback on your own credibility. Express your gratitude if they accept. Graciously allow them to decline, if that's their choice, without their needing to explain themselves.

5. Explain both the grid and the follow-up questions. Give them their copy of this filled-in dashboard. Suggest a date for returning their feedback.

6. Again, invite them to be absolutely candid. Express your appreciation in advance.

Guiding Principles Dashboard

Name: _____

I would like you to give me some feedback on the strength of my guiding principles and values. In the grid below, I have written the guiding principles and values that I aspire to embody in my everyday behaviors, words and choices.

Please think back on our interactions or your observations of me in the past few weeks.

With what frequency do my behaviors, words and choices *regularly* demonstrate the principles that I have written below? The key is *regularly*.

Seldom	Sometimes	About Half the Time	Often	Almost Always
①	②	③	④	⑤

My Guiding Principles and Values	Behaviors	Words	Choices
EXAMPLE Value: *Diversity* This means: *I include individuals with diverse experiences and knowledge on my projects.* *I actively seek out differing points of view before making important choices.* *I insist on and support the members of my group for doing the same.*	4	5	3
Ⓐ Value: 　　This means:			

Copyright © 2011 by Bridge Group Communications, LLC. All rights reserved.

Name: _____

		About		Almost
Seldom	Sometimes	Half the Time	Often	Always
①	②	③	④	⑤

My Guiding Principles and Values	Behaviors	Words	Choices
B Value: This means:			
C Value: This means:			
D Value: This means:			
E Value: This means:			

Copyright © 2011 by Bridge Group Communications, LLC. All rights reserved.

Name: _____

Seldom	Sometimes	About Half the Time	Often	Almost Always
①	②	③	④	⑤

My Guiding Principles and Values	Behaviors	Words	Choices
F Value: This means:			
G Value: This means:			
H Value: This means:			
I Value: This means:			

Copyright © 2011 by Bridge Group Communications, LLC. All rights reserved.

Name: _____

		About		**Almost**
Seldom	**Sometimes**	**Half the Time**	**Often**	**Always**
①	②	③	④	⑤

My Guiding Principles and Values	Behaviors	Words	Choices
Ⓙ Value: This means:			

On a separate page, please answer the following questions for each item that you marked below 4 on the dashboard:

1. Why did you not give this item a score of 4 to 5?
2. What would I need to be doing differently for you to raise the score to a 4 or a 5?

Finally, please let me know if there are any *other* principles — good, bad or indifferent — that you would say *regularly* guide the ways in which I behave, talk with others, make choices and generally interact with you and others in the community.

Please return no later than _____
write in date

Return information:

Thank you for your participation and candor. I'm very grateful.

Copyright © 2011 by Bridge Group Communications, LLC. All rights reserved.

Exercise: Thank Others for Their Feedback

Once you've gotten the feedback, close the loop by having a face-to-face or phone conversation to say once again how much you appreciate the other person's courage and friendship in offering their feedback and comments.

This conversation also provides a place for you to ask for any clarification that might help you more fully understand what others have offered to you.

Here are a few guidelines that will help you honor the courage and friendship that the other person has shown you as you have this conversation:

1. If you need to ask for clarification in order to better understand their feedback and rating, keep your questions open-ended. For example, "What did you mean by . . . ?" (*and* follow guideline #3, below).
2. Ask: "What could I do differently or more frequently to live up to the values that I aspire to embody?" (*and* follow guideline #3).
3. Do not justify, excuse, say "but" or in any way push back. Your only goal is to hear the person out and gather good data.
4. Say, "Thank you."
5. Let the responses incubate in your mind for a while before drawing any conclusions.

Growth and Mastery

Now it is time to come full circle and allow yourself to arrive, once again, at a place of personal introspection (looking inside) and reflection (considering everything that others have told you). Once more, I draw on the wisdom of a valued mentor who pushed me to grow by saying, "You cannot be everything to everyone, *but* what part of what they are saying might be true?"

What do you make of all the **information, knowledge and understanding** that you have gathered — all the data that is swirling around in your head? Specifically: How does your self-assessment compare to what others have shared with you about yourself?

See PDF Worksheet p. 34

The Citizen Leader: Be the Person You'd Want to Follow

Exercise: Seek Insight

Insight is a shift in perception that allows you to comprehend more completely the inner nature of things. In our case here, I am asking you to seek insight about *your* inner nature as you compare your self-assessment with the feedback from others. You might experience insight as sudden clarity, a keener focus, an unexpected revelation. Whatever the case, insight is neither good nor bad. Insight is not a judgment. Instead, insight is *a better understanding, a fuller understanding* — perhaps even a substantially different or unexpected understanding.

Be curious.

Ask yourself: *What is the message here?*

Be humble as you seek insight.

Keep an open mind and an open heart as you look over the data and comments.

Allow for a shift in your own perception about yourself.

If you find yourself experiencing some initial confusion or discomfort as you compare your self-assessment with the feedback you've gotten from others, that's normal. It is also normal for your mind (more specifically, your ego) to distance itself from the cause of that confusion or discomfort — in this case, that very same feedback from others. If you find *that* happening, take a break and come back to it later. But do come back to it rather than allow any anxious reaction to minimize the effort you've gone through or rob you of the possibility to understand more fully *who you are*. Such was the case with the two managers I talked about earlier. In attempting to dismiss the feedback they had gathered from their staff, they opted to remain blind to parts of themselves that the people around them clearly saw. Even more damaging, they robbed themselves of the chance to hear the ideas those people might have offered to help them grow as human beings, as leaders and as citizens in their communities outside of work. *And* that is why I ask you to be patient, and remind you that as you take in the feedback, compare your assessments and seek insight, you do so with curiosity and humility.

Now to you. Considering all the information and knowledge you have gathered and the feedback others have shared with you:

What *better and fuller understanding* do you have about the character that resides at your core?

See PDF Worksheet p. 35

What *better and fuller understanding* do you have about who you are in others' eyes?

See PDF Worksheet p. 35

Exercise: Who Am I?

Now, equipped with your own insights — discerned from the feedback given to you by your colleagues and the members of your community — you have "good data" (that is, objective data) on the values and principles that *they* regularly observe by the pattern of your actions.

Using all the data that you have collected in the prior pages — your own and theirs — write down once again what you honestly believe are the *handful* of values and principles that you actually demonstrate regularly in your behaviors, word and choices.

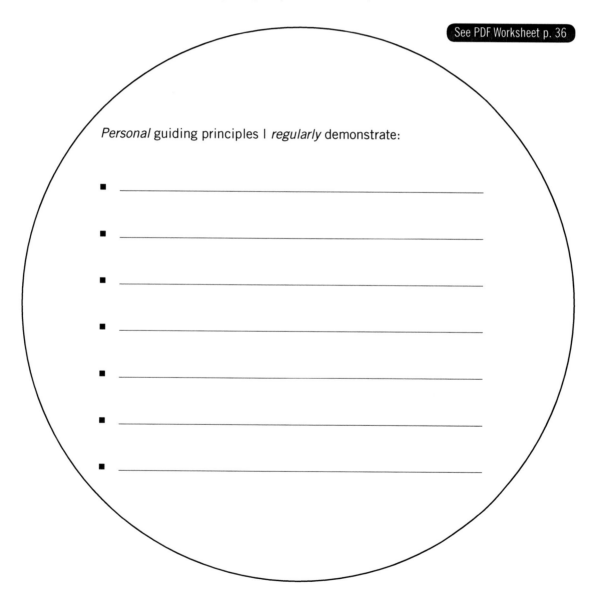

See PDF Worksheet p. 36

Personal guiding principles I *regularly* demonstrate:

- _____

- _____

- _____

- _____

- _____

- _____

- _____

If at this point you find that you still have more than a handful of guiding principles and values, then go through a second iteration in the following way:

1. Taking each principle in turn, remove it from the set of values that you've chosen.

2. Now ask yourself, in doing so:
   - *Do I feel that I am ripping away at the very fabric of my being?*
   - *Do I feel that I am stripping myself of part of who I am, in action or word?*
   - If the answer to one or both is a resounding "Yes," that's good data! Sounds like a keeper.

3. But is it? Prove it to yourself, just one more time.
   - Look back over the past few weeks at your behaviors and choices — at your life at home, at work and in your community. Ask yourself: *Were my actions, interactions and decisions (even when no one else was looking) a reflection of this principle?*
   - Whatever the answer, you'll have some good data to guide you in discerning whether this one is a keeper — that is, whether it is one that lies at your core — or whether, perhaps, it is one to which you aspire.

Who you are speaks to me so loudly that I can hardly hear what you are saying."

— Ralph Waldo Emerson

Exercise: Who or How Do I Aspire to Be?

When we are in touch with our truth (good, bad or indifferent), we are living more from our core. In this chapter, you have sought to do just that — to be in touch with your truth. You have endeavored to uncover and express an authentic response to the question: *Who am I?* Along the way, you have drawn on your powers of introspection, reflection and curiosity to look inside and at yourself. Exercising your humility, you have gathered information from people around you and sought insights from their feedback about the qualities at your core. Now, you arrive at a point where, equipped with your truth, you can look to the future and ask:

Who or how do I aspire to be (that is different from who or how I am today)?

Why do I care?

What are my concerns or reservations about whether this is possible?

What do I need to do in the future to grow in integrity?

What do I need to do to grow in credibility?

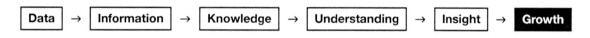

Spend time pondering these questions with whole-minded curiosity, and welcome the responses that percolate to the surface with wholehearted humility. **Seek** insight in your responses — that is, look for a shift in perception that gives you a better and fuller understanding of your core, the person you aspire to be, and why. Your insight will help you **decide** on priorities for your continued growth as a human being, as a citizen and as a leader in your community. Finally, **commit** yourself to a regular practice of behaving and acting in ways that will contribute to your *being* that person. It is this regular practice that leads to **mastery** — mastery of both your personal integrity and your credibility. The reward that you reap over time will be a life that has more and greater **meaning** — a life that enriches your spirits and those of the people around you.

Now, to you:

Who or how do I aspire to *be* (that is different from who or how I am today)?

See PDF Worksheet p. 37

Why do I care?

See PDF Worksheet p. 37

What are my concerns or reservations about whether this is possible?

See PDF Worksheet p. 37

What do I need to do in the future to grow in integrity?

See PDF Worksheet p. 38

What do I need to do to grow in credibility?

See PDF Worksheet p. 38

When you say and do those things that are consistent with the principles and values that you hold most dear and aspire to in life, you are taking *principle-guided action*. Indeed, if your point of departure as you set out in pursuit of what you want (i.e., your goals, objectives, desires) is to reaffirm your commitment to your principles and values, *and* if, as a result, you do and say only those things that are consistent with your values and principles, then your actions are and will be principle guided.

Yet it will come as no surprise to you if I say: We live in a world where it is tempting (sometimes encouraged, supported, even required) to focus more on what we want to have, or accomplish or experience, and then to say or do whatever seems needed to make it happen. Ours is a world in which the ends often justify the means, or, in real terms, where profit or power (or both) often take precedence over principle.

Since, in the most real way, what we say and what we do defines us, the important question is: *Are you being the person you want to be — the person you want to live with?* The real work of creating a life of meaning is to be the self you want to live with, rather than being a self you end up *having* to live with or, worse, a self you cannot stand.

> *As to methods there may be a million and then some, but principles are few. The man who grasps principles can successfully select his own methods. The man who tries methods, ignoring principles, is sure to have trouble."*
>
> — Ralph Waldo Emerson

Cheating Yourself

All judgment aside, I've grown to accept that cheating is probably part of the human condition — good, bad or indifferent. Sometimes we are the ones who are doing the cheating. Sometimes we are the ones being cheated. Either way, cheating eventually (if not immediately) injures both the cheater and the cheated.

The following examples illustrate the many and varied definitions of the word **cheat**:

I cheat myself when I **blunt the effect of** my diet by eating more than my prescribed 2,500 calories a day.

A teenager cheats when she **violates the rules of** copyright protection by copying a friend's CD or software onto her computer.

A college student cheats when he **defeats the purpose of** a term paper by paying someone else to write it.

A teacher cheats a student when she **deprives her of full information** about a controversial topic, and thereby prevents her from making clear and informed decisions and choices for herself. The same can be said of a parent and child.

An employee cheats when he defrauds his employer by **making a false claim** on his expense report or time card.

A manager cheats when she **leads us to believe, by behaviors and words that she knows to be insincere**, that a decision is entirely up to us — only to veto it or change it if it is not the decision she expects.

A corporation (or any taxpayer) cheats when it **defrauds** the U.S. Treasury by misrepresenting its taxable income.

An athlete cheats when he **violates the rules of** the sport by taking prohibited, performance-enhancing supplements.

Friends, public figures and spiritual leaders cheat when they are **sexually unfaithful** to their partners or spouses.

A government cheats when it **leads us by deceit** into war.

We are what we repeatedly do."

— Aristotle

While the severity of injury caused by cheating depends on the circumstances — superficial, shallow, profound, grave — no sustained injury is harmless. At their most grave, repeated acts of heinous cheating (like the systematic deceit about WMDs that led us into the Iraq War) cause death. Yet, even at the lesser extreme, a superficial injury like a paper cut, if experienced daily, makes for a painful existence. As for the points in between, when we cheat on ourselves or others, the injuries we cause contribute to an already existing population of wounded spirits, wounded emotions and wounded bodies.

Of immediate concern to our exploration of and commitment to guiding principles is this: When *you or I* repeatedly cheat on our values, and when *we* injure and reinjure ourselves or others in so doing, we join (or more deeply entrench ourselves among) the ranks of the walking wounded.

Personally, I've had my fill of being cheated, but I expect more to come — I would be naïve to think otherwise. More important, I've had my fill of doing the cheating, too — of self-inflicted injury — despite its short-term benefits and payoffs. I've learned that eventually the damage does add up or the truth does come out, and in the longer term, I pay out much more in reparations or wreckage to my reputation than I ever reaped in the first place.

But that realization didn't come early on. It came slowly over time, through trial and error, and after a few devastating blows that I delivered to myself. Then as now, I live in a world in which some of our elders, our purported role models and too often our culture itself turn a blind eye to cheating, on condition that it helps achieve desired goals — profit, power, prestige, position, personal pleasure, personal gain. I've tried my hand at that approach, believing that is how the game is played. And I have crashed terribly, and have writhed in pain as I felt my integrity and credibility ripped to shreds *at my own hand* by attempting to game the system for my own benefit.

Honesty in action and word come much more naturally to me now by way of routine adherence to the guiding principle — *dare to be true*. I strive to make it the basis of my behaviors. I endeavor to conduct myself from a place of knowing and owning how *I want to be* in the world, regardless of how anyone else might choose to act or be (or want me to act or be). Mind you, my execution is not perfect. There are still the occasional paper cuts, and even flesh wounds. So, perfection aside, I strive for excellence — and that is a standard I want to meet every day.

You should be the change you want to see in the world."
— Mohandas Gandhi

Exercise: Principle-Guided Action

The more we commit to live by way of principle-guided action — that is, the more we intentionally act in ways that reflect the person we aspire to be, even when it's difficult to do so — the more we live lives that have greater meaning.

So I come back to you, your thoughts on who or how you aspire to be in the world and what you will do or say regularly to be that person.

JUMP IN

*To grow in integrity and credibility, and to become the person I aspire to be, I **commit** to demonstrate my principles more regularly by way of these specific behaviors and actions.*

Guiding Principles	Specific Behaviors and Actions
EXAMPLE • *Dare to be true*	*I acknowledge that greed, a sense of entitlement, envy or financial fear can and will tempt me to bend the truth at times. When it does, I will opt for truth.* *I pay for my music and software downloads, and do not copy them from a friend or colleague.* *I annotate my writing, giving credit to authors or sources when I quote their words or from their work.*

Since what we choose is who we are,
And what we love we yet shall be,
The goal may ever shine afar —
The will to reach it makes us free."

— William DeWitt Hyde, President,
Bowdoin College, 1885–1917

Guiding Principles	Specific Behaviors and Actions

Guiding Principles	Specific Behaviors and Actions

Guiding Principles	Specific Behaviors and Actions

Guiding Principles	Specific Behaviors and Actions

Guiding Principles	Specific Behaviors and Actions

Guiding Principles	Specific Behaviors and Actions

Legacy

My grandfather came over on the boat from Sicily at the age of 20, landed at Ellis Island in New York Harbor on April 30, 1900, settled among his Italian relatives in Brooklyn and set up shop as a barber. Four years later, he married a Sicilian farm girl, newly arrived in America from his home village of Juliana in the mountains above Palermo. He was naturalized as an American citizen on May 6, 1905. My grandmother gave birth to four children — three boys and a girl — and my grandfather made sure his family never wanted for food or shelter, in no small part because he had a great mind for numbers and regularly won at pinochle. He and the other Italian men in the neighborhood would play the game for hours after work. Several times a week, he'd use part of the winnings to buy ice cream or pastries at the corner German bakery for his kids. He'd help out his brothers and cousins with a loan when they asked. He'd take half a day off on Sundays to be with the family; otherwise he was in his shop.

At least, that's the story that I was told by my uncle and my aunt. I repeat it because I like it. It is a pioneering, self-assured, make-your-own-way-in-the-world American story. Support a family by day by the labor of your hands, and by playing and winning at cards at night — it sounds tough. Treat the kids, and help out the relatives — it sounds tender. Work your tail off to provide, because that is our lot and we embrace it — it sounds noble.

But that is all I really know about my grandfather. He died before I was born, and my father never really talked much about him. So all I have to go on are these sound bites: *provided for his family, always put food on the table, good at cards, a pioneer, gutsy and principled.* That is the only memory of my grandfather to survive today. And since I am the only one of my generation to have heard these stories, I doubt that much, if anything at all, about my grandfather will survive beyond the tomorrow of my life.

I don't know that my grandfather gave much thought to how he wanted to be remembered, or that he cared about being remembered at all. I suspect that he had his hands full just getting from one day to the next. As he lived and toiled and took care of his family, my grandfather was just being who he was. His memory would take care of itself. He died in 1953. History has all but forgotten him.

I doubt that much if anything about my life (or my interests or accomplishments, or failures for that matter) will survive beyond the brief memories of my contemporaries.

And what is remembered of me will take on a different form for the many people with whom I crossed paths along the way: parents, partners, lovers, friends, teachers, teammates, therapists, colleagues, coworkers, children, caregivers, casual acquaintances . . . the list can go on for pages. What is certain is that in the minds of most, the sound bites are all pretty much set. There is little that I can do to recast the image or impression that I have already left. And so while I might wonder, "How do I want to be remembered?" the reality is that in the fleeting moments that I might be recalled to mind at all, I will be remembered in ways that I can neither control nor change.

I used to get unduly wrapped up in the idea that I needed to leave a legacy. I used to feel pressured to be memorable or to do things that would be memorable. I don't any longer. I don't want the pressure. I don't need the pressure on top of just getting from one day to the next. I know more clearly now that the memory of me and my life, like that of my grandfather, will prove to be little more than a handful of sound bites, remembered by few, spoken of seldom and forgotten too soon.

What a relief.

Now, I get on with the life I have in front of me, one day at a time. And I get on with my life with presence and with deliberate purpose. Sure, I still sometimes ponder, "How do I want to be remembered?" But much more often, I ask myself, "How do I want to *be*?" I focus less on *when I am gone*, and more on *as I am, today*. I try to pay attention to the right here, the right now — to the moments that, of their own accord, and without any help from me, coalesce into the hours, the days and the years of my life, today. I pay attention to my behaviors, my words and my choices that of their own accord show me who I am today. *And* I try to live the behaviors and words and choices that help me to be the person I strive to be, today.

I have grown to cherish the sacred nature of this work.

Living with Integrity in My Community

Values of My Community

Let's conclude our exploration of integrity and credibility by examining the values of your community, and your relationship to those values.

Community values — or shared values — are the promises that we make to one another about how we will act and interact. Shared values hold a community together, whether it be a family, friends, a fellowship, neighbors, a virtual network, a town, a team, a troop, a company, a country or a culture. Shared values are our glue. When we collectively adhere to a set of shared principles about how we will act and interact with one another, we strengthen our bond as a community. Conversely, when we fail to adhere to our shared values, we weaken our communal bond — we become unglued.

At the extreme, when there is no set of values that are commonly shared *and* actively observed by the members of a community, there is no community. There is, perhaps, a collection of individuals who inhabit the same space and time but who (understandably) are acting in their own self-interest, often in ways that serve to keep them apart from one another rather than create the bonds that hold them together as a part of a whole.

Let's take a look at *your* communities. Begin by considering them all. Think about the various bands and crowds with whom you come together (real or virtual) to support and serve one another. Choose one. It could be the one that you proclaimed yourself a proud member of when we first started to explore the meaning of community in the earlier chapter, or it could be any other community that is particularly influential in your life.

Which one of your communities do you choose?

See PDF Worksheet p. 42

Exercise: Values of My Community — Identify

For the community that you have chosen, take some time to consider how you would answer the questions below. If it helps, over the next few days observe other members of your community while you ponder these questions. As you do so, remember that by emphasizing *regularly*, I am asking you to look for the pattern rather than the occasional quality that is suggested by people's actions. When your observations have provided you with enough good data, write down your conclusions.

What are the values or guiding principles that most accurately describe the way individuals in my community *regularly* behave toward one another?

See PDF Worksheet p. 43

The Citizen Leader: Be the Person You'd Want to Follow

What are the values or guiding principles that most accurately describe the way individuals in my community *regularly* speak with one another?

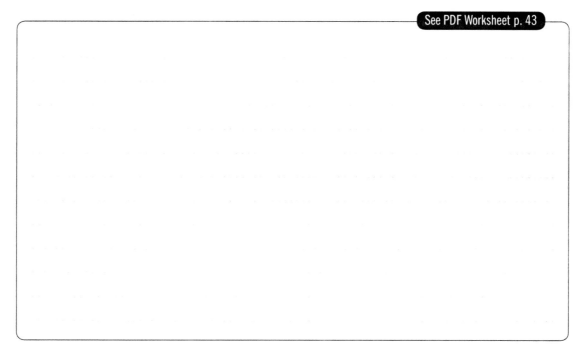

See PDF Worksheet p. 43

What are the values or guiding principles that *most frequently* influence the choices people make in our community?

See PDF Worksheet p. 44

What are the values or guiding principles that *most frequently* influence the decisions people make?

See PDF Worksheet p. 44

What are the values or guiding principles that *most frequently* influence the actions people take?

See PDF Worksheet p. 44

Exercise: Values of My Community — Define

Based on the observations and experiences that you recorded on the previous pages, write below what you consider to be the essential *handful* of shared values of your community, and how those values are *regularly* expressed in action.

EXAMPLE

Community: Let me take one community of which I am a member — the colleagues with whom I collaborate and conduct leadership workshops.

Value: We appreciate and look out for one another.

How this is *regularly* expressed in action:

- If one of us is ill and unable to conduct a workshop, another jumps in to do so, even if it means flying cross-country, giving up days of a weekend or sacrificing some personal plans.
- We give one another candid feedback, we compliment good work and we speak well of one another.
- I share with them the materials in my book as I write. They give me thoughtful feedback, all the while maintaining confidentiality.
- We often celebrate one another's birthdays and other annual holidays by organizing small gatherings or dinners.

I recognize that some of the community values you uncovered might be inconsistent with your personal values, or might even be what you consider to be "negative" values. If that's the truth, then that's good data. Good, bad or indifferent, what you are looking for here are the actual, core shared values of your community: those that are acted out most *regularly*.

Value:

See PDF Worksheet p. 45

How it is *regularly* expressed in action:

See PDF Worksheet p. 45

Value:

See PDF Worksheet p. 45

How it is *regularly* expressed in action:

See PDF Worksheet p. 46

Value:

See PDF Worksheet p. 46

How it is *regularly* expressed in action:

See PDF Worksheet p. 46

Value:

See PDF Worksheet p. 46

How it is *regularly* expressed in action:

See PDF Worksheet p. 47

Value:

See PDF Worksheet p. 47

How it is *regularly* expressed in action:

See PDF Worksheet p. 47

Exercise: Community Values Dashboard — Self-Assessment

Use this *Community Values Dashboard* to assess the strength of your:

1. engagement with those values and
2. adherence to those values.

You can measure the strength of your *engagement* by assessing both:

- the degree to which you really **know** what each value means (I ask you to gauge this by how clearly you can explain its meaning to someone else) and
- the degree to which you say that you **care** about and support the value.

You can measure the strength of your *adherence* to the values by assessing:

- the degree to which you **act** in ways that regularly demonstrate the value.

On the grid that follows: (See PDF Worksheet p. 48)

1. Write each of the *handful* of your community's shared values. (You do not need to use all of the rows if you have identified fewer than five shared values.)

2. Then, assess honestly how much you agree with each of these three statements:
   - Know: I can clearly explain the meaning of this value to someone else in our community.
   - Care: I personally care about and support this value.
   - Act: My behaviors, words and actions *regularly* demonstrate this value. The key word is *regularly*.

	Strongly Disagree ①	Disagree ②	Neutral ③	Agree ④	Strongly Agree ⑤

Our Community Values	Know	Care	Act
EXAMPLE Value: *We appreciate and look out for one another.*	4	5	3
Value:			
Value:			
Value:			
Value:			
Value:			

Exercise: Living with Integrity (I)

You started this chapter, "Living with Integrity in My Community," by considering a series of questions to help you identify the shared values — the glue — of your chosen community. Then, you assessed the strength of your personal engagement with those values, and your adherence to them. Now, let's move on to the questions that get to the heart of the matter: whether you are indeed *living with integrity* in the community that you have chosen.

First let's be clear about what this means. In the previous chapter, we talked at length about the notion that integrity is, first and foremost, living from the core. It is behaving, speaking and acting in ways that are consistent with the guiding principles and values that you commit to — the guiding principles and values that help you grow in credibility. In principle, it should make little difference what the values are of the community you find yourself in.

Your ability to live from the core is made easier when the values of your community align with your own — when the promises that the members of the community make to one another about how they will act and interact agree with the promises you make to yourself about how you will behave, speak and act.

For instance, I just shared with you that one of the values of my community of professional leadership trainers is *we appreciate and look out for one another*. I consider that this aligns with my personal values of *connection* and *do good work in service of the common good* that I shared and explained earlier. The wording is different, to be sure, but as I think about the spirit that underlies these values, I am comfortable with saying that the behaviors and actions that originate from my core are consistent with the values of my community.

Now to you. Given the work that you just completed to identify and define the values of your chosen community, let's look to where you are in agreement — that is, where it is easy for you to live with integrity, to live from your core.

Take some time to examine both sets of values — yours and those of your community — and then jot down your thoughts about where, how and why the two are most aligned with one another.

See PDF Worksheet p. 49

The Citizen Leader: Be the Person You'd Want to Follow

Exercise: Living with Integrity (II) — Strengthening My Bond with My Community

Now, let's move on to the second element of living with integrity in your community — that is, your committing to adhere *regularly*, through your actions, to the shared values of your community that might not figure into your own set of principles. The understanding, mind you, is that those values are consistent with your own. More emphatically, the prerequisite is that your community's values do not require you to relinquish the promises that you make to yourself — to behave or act in ways that violate your principles.

On the *Community Values Dashboard*, you assessed the degree to which your behaviors, words and actions *regularly* demonstrate each one of your community's values. An "act" score of 4 to 5 reflects strong adherence — the degree to which you *act* in ways that regularly demonstrate the value. More importantly, an "act" score of 4 to 5 shows you what and where the glue is that bonds you with the other members of your community.

Perhaps there were values for which you gave yourself a lower "act" score. That, too, is good data. Don't feel a need to attach any judgment to the score. Instead, applaud yourself for your honesty and candor.

For instance, at home, in the small community that my partner CJ and I make up together, one of our shared values is *collaboration*. In our case, collaboration is understood to mean actively inviting the other into a conversation about any project that touches us both from the get-go. This has included home and garden improvements, vacation and holiday plans and the like. Now there is nothing about our definition of collaboration that is antithetical to who I am or who I aspire to be. That's the good news. The bad news is that I would give myself a score of "2" in terms of my *regularly* demonstrating behavior and actions that support collaboration. Here's why. While I do welcome and value the input that my partner offers, I often wait to seek out his counsel or ideas until after I have fully fleshed out my own. I am more inclined to act independently, rather than collaboratively from the beginning of a project, and then engage with him only too late, with what can feel like a done deal. As a result, at times, I set myself apart from him, perhaps making him feel that I do not respect his intelligence and creativity, and maybe even causing him to be wary of my motives. Not a good plan for building a strong sense of community at home. And I would venture, not a good plan for *any* community. I am still working on greater adherence to collaboration.

Going back to your data, use it to help you target where you want or need to strengthen your bonds with your community. To ignore your data or put off incorporating it into your behavior until some other time is to risk weakening or undermining those bonds. More frequently, in your daily behaviors and actions, commit to demonstrating the community values for which you gave yourself a lower "act" score. As you do so, you will help yourself become more a part of your community, and just as importantly, you will help strengthen the community as a whole.

Respond to these three questions, and follow through with action:

Which community values or guiding principles must I make the effort to adhere to more closely to strengthen my bond with my community?

See PDF Worksheet p. 50

I care to make the effort because . . .

See PDF Worksheet p. 50

What specific behaviors and actions will I demonstrate *regularly* (*or more regularly*) in order to adhere more closely to these community values?

See PDF Worksheet p. 51

Exercise: Living with Integrity (III)

Finally, let's address the third element of living with integrity in your community, that is, acting from your core — adhering to your own set of principles — when one or more of your community's values offends, prompts or, worse, requires you to violate your own values.

Which of your community's values, if any, seems to be at odds with your guiding principles?

See PDF Worksheet p. 52

Why are they at odds?

See PDF Worksheet p. 52

How do you handle it when one (or more) of the shared values of your community seems to be at odds with your guiding principles?

See PDF Worksheet p. 52

This above all: to thine own self be true,
And it must follow, as the night the day,
Thou canst not then be false to any man."

— Shakespeare

It's Up to Me

I do not ask the last question on the previous page lightly. Once again, "What do you do when your guiding principles seem to stand at odds with the shared values of your community?" I do not presume to believe that the answer is easy, either. Yet, the question is one that people struggle with every day.

Let me offer a few approaches from among a spectrum of possible responses. I draw these from my personal and professional life:

- The slam dunk,
- The dilemma,
- The defining choice, and
- The defying choice.

Whichever *your* approach, it is up to you.

The Slam Dunk

At 97 years old, my Uncle Anthony didn't hesitate for a moment to share the principles that had guided him through eight decades of his adult life. Picture this: his caregiver, Joy, had just gently combed his hair, and I remarked how fortunate he was to have someone so nice looking after him. He added, "Yes, and she is so very pretty too." I jokingly replied, "Careful, Anthony — Joy is married." Without missing a beat, he cracked, "But she has a younger sister." I tried to be witty and cracked back, "Keep it legal, pal." It was just our usual good-humored banter. Yet, on this occasion, without any prompting from me, Anthony paused, and with great presence continued, "I always have. That's how I've lived my life." I couldn't resist, so I asked him to say more about what was going through his mind. What he said in the next moment has become a memory that I will treasure for a long time. With ease and with a solid sense of self, my uncle said, quite simply, "I have lived by three principles my whole life: I never tell a lie. I always pay my taxes on time. And I never get in trouble with the law."

Simple, clear, incisive. And each one a clear and true reflection of the man.

I never tell a lie. I never knew Uncle Anthony to say anything that he knew to be untrue. Oh sure, in our conversations, he had said things that were wrong or misinformed. We all do. But I had never known him to *knowingly misrepresent.*

I always pay my taxes on time. I have every confidence that he did. Yet, there was much more to this simple idea, much more that reflected a larger principle at play. Anthony knew what his obligations were to the people in his various and often overlapping communities, and he accepted and met those obligations head-on and without begrudging them. When he made a promise, he kept it. When he made a commitment, he followed through. When he assumed responsibility out of his own initiative, he persevered.

I never get in trouble with the law. And, to my knowledge, he never did — not even a speeding ticket. Yet once again, his words only touched the surface of a broader value that all who knew him witnessed regularly and routinely. Anthony had a solid, personal sense of what right action was, and what it was not. No one was going to tell him differently. Yes, there were those who disagreed with him. I certainly did, on occasion. Regardless, he relied on an internal gyroscope to stay true to his sense of right action every day. Whether in his professional life as an accountant, at home in a marriage of 52 years, in his community as a volunteer on the finance committees of his sports club and condo association or as the patriarch of an extended family of nephews and nieces (three generations' worth!), my uncle played by a succinct set of rules. If challenged to act differently by the influences or the winds swirling around him, however tempting or menacing those winds might be, for Anthony Alduino, the answer to *What do I do?* was a slam dunk: Anthony did it his way.

The Dilemma

Anthony grew up in Brooklyn, New York, among a community of immigrant parents and first-generation American kids, an environment much influenced by a culture of *family.*

Many individuals with whom I have worked over the years profess to pattern their behaviors and choices after an adherence to *family.* When I've asked them to explain, they have shared stories that show vastly different definitions of what *family* looks like in action. Among those differences:

- For some it means *spending time with family* — that is, regularly making choices that permit them to be with members of their family.
- For others it means *providing for family* — in other words, engaging in activities that provide for the maintenance and welfare of the family.

Of course, there is no correct or right or singular definition of *family*, just as there is no singular definition of many, if not most, principles or values. What *is* important, though, is that with regard to the handful of principles that you attach to, you make the effort to develop definitions that resonate with you and that inform you in your interactions with the world around you.

I cannot promise that it will be easy to settle on a clear definition. Deciphering and deciding from among many differing interpretations will pose its challenges, if not its dilemmas, just as the concept of *family* does. Nor can I promise you that it will be easy living by a definition once you have settled on it. Much to the contrary, you can expect to run up against community or cultural or workplace values that conflict with your own and that seem to force you to choose between competing concerns. This is the nature of dilemma: having to make a choice from among one or several alternatives, each of which presents some upside and some downside. For example, let's say that you hold to *spending time with family* as a personal value. Meanwhile, suppose that *teamwork* is one of the principles in your work community. It is almost predictable that occasionally the two will clash, both competing for your presence and your time — both laying claim to your choices. We see and feel much confusion, even consternation, about how to balance the two in contemporary culture.

Suffice it to say that you will encounter dilemmas along the way. There is no ideal path to follow as you navigate through. Your choices will be individual and situational. My hope is that they will be well considered and consistent with who you strive to be. This will be especially important — and an even stronger imperative — when:

- dilemma pits personal principles against community values in ways that simply do not or cannot accommodate a balancing act, *or*
- dilemma pits personal principles against personal desires (or wants) in a way that, by definition, one must give way to the other.

The Defining Choice

A dilemma can bring you to a tipping point where you can consciously choose to define (or perhaps redefine) both yourself and your life.

Let me illustrate. Ten years ago, I was part of a small team of consultants and facilitators conducting leadership development seminars for clients throughout the country and all over the world. This required a ton of travel — another airport, another plane, another hotel, another dinner alone. And while it was up to each of us to choose whether to take on yet another client, culturally our explicit principles of *teamwork* and *client delight* translated into an implicit understanding that we would *only sparingly say no*. Each time I acquiesced to that cultural value, each time I said yes even though I really wanted to say no, I was choosing to be away from home. That choice chronically bumped up against my personal value that I would *make healthy choices for mind, body and spirit* (which included choosing to spend time with friends and to focus on forming a primary relationship). While I cared greatly for the other members of my team, and I was devoted to doing great work for our clients, I also deeply wanted to strengthen my friendships and settle with a partner (both of which required face-time at home). I had lived with the dilemma for many years.

It was mid-September when this chronic dilemma grabbed hold of me hard and offered me yet another choice between the competing values. I had just returned to work from having taken a two-month unpaid leave of absence into which I had tried to cram what I hoped would be a sufficient amount of face-time with friends to satisfy my longings to strengthen my relationships, and maybe even create new ones. I had also hoped that my sabbatical would help me establish a healthier balance between my personal principle to *make healthy choices for my body, mind and spirit* and the workplace values of *teamwork* and *client delight*. Yet, in the first few days after my return, I was asked to take on client engagements that would require nine back-to-back weeks of travel.

So, while I might have taken a break, my dilemma hadn't budged, and it met me square-on upon my return. What to do?

I could go back to saying yes, even though I really wanted to say no, or I could choose to be the person I was striving to be. (Have you heard Einstein's observation that *insanity is defined as doing the same thing the same way you've always done it, and expecting to get different results?*) Well, I chose to do things differently this time around. I made a choice in favor of *making healthy choices for my mind, body and spirit*. I ultimately decided to resign. More to the point, I decided to make the saner choice: to remove myself from a culture whose values caused me too frequently to minimize my own. I have never regretted that decision, never.

The Defying Choice

Finally, let's look at what happens if someone in a position of influence or power — someone higher in the chain of command — tells you to do something that runs contrary to your guiding principles (and cloaks that demand in the cloth of cultural values).

Here's an example — an encounter that upset me at the time, and still upsets me now as I write about it. I was working with two individuals, both of them intelligent professionals in the high-tech field, who had recently been confronted with the dilemma of having to choose between personal integrity and professional loyalty. One insisted that while our examination of personal integrity and its connection to public credibility was all fine and good, it just was not the "real world." He went on to explain that in his short tenure at his company, he had learned that it was best not to contradict the boss, but instead to simply do as he was told. The second person chimed in that she felt the same way. She followed that by sharing that her boss had told her to misrepresent test results so that a project could proceed uninterrupted, and rationalized his demand by saying they would fix the shortcomings later. She believed that she needed to acquiesce so as to show *loyalty*, and that not to do so would be seen as a liability to her career. She felt pressured by a seeming cultural norm for loyalty to compromise her core. At the time, she was only in her mid-20s.

Regrettably, all too often I witness this insidious insistence on loyalty (or other cultural imperatives such as *conformity, shareholder value, victory, security* and the like, any of which can suffocate personal principles). I regularly read and hear about its showing up in business and government in stories portraying individuals who have drifted away from their core to pursue power, profit, prestige, position, pleasure or personal gain. I observe it in the behaviors and words of individuals whose playbook for *their real world* parallels the philosophy that *"Principle is okay, up to a certain point, but principle doesn't do any good if you lose."*[2]

To acquiesce to a show of *loyalty (or conformity, shareholder value, victory, security,* and so on) at the expense of your core values causes injury to your character — an injury that can be a lasting liability to your career *and* your conscience.

---

2. Campaign advice given by former Vice President Dick Cheney to associates when he was White House chief of staff. Source: *Worse Than Watergate: The Secret Presidency of George W. Bush*, by John W. Dean.

I take heart in the words of Thomas Jefferson: *". . . in matters of style, swim with the current; in matters of principle, stand like a rock . . ."*

And I find courage in the wisdom of Mohandas Gandhi: *"A 'No' uttered from the deepest conviction is better than a 'Yes' merely uttered to please or, worse, to avoid trouble."*

It takes real courage to defy someone, especially if that someone else is in a position to deny you something you desire. We are right back to dilemma. Or are we? By making the choice to defy someone else's demand that you damn your own character, you safeguard the only thing that you can truly call yours — your integrity.

It's up to you. In the end, you are the final arbiter of your actions.

Co-Creator

In the end, you are the final arbiter of your actions. In the end, your daily behaviors, words and choices help shape the character of your community for yourself, your family, friends, colleagues, coworkers and your fellow citizens. You are not alone in this endeavor, but you are singularly the owner of your actions, and responsible for their influence and impact — positive or negative — on the character of the communities in which you live and work.

Consider, then, the power of this role as a co-creator of your world. When you live with integrity, you help to shape a world that reflects the principles you hold dear. As for the opposite, think of the implications. When you behave and act in ways that *do not* reflect your core, you help shape a world that mirrors whatever *other* values you are demonstrating — positive or otherwise.

You have given considerable thought to your community over the course of this chapter. Be the co-creator. Help shape a world that reflects the principles you hold dear. Let the questions and exercise on the next few pages prompt you and guide you as you strive to strengthen the character of your community.

First, ask yourself this: Is there a shared value or guiding principle that we — the members of the community — must strive to adhere to more closely in the next twelve to eighteen months?

Which shared value or guiding principle must *we* strive to adhere to?

See PDF Worksheet p. 53

Why is it important for us to adhere more closely to this value?

See PDF Worksheet p. 53

Second, ask yourself this: Is there any other value or guiding principle that we would be well served to adopt and adhere to in the next twelve to eighteen months?

Define the value or principle:

> See PDF Worksheet p. 54

Why is it important for us to adhere to this value?

> See PDF Worksheet p. 54

The Citizen Leader: Be the Person You'd Want to Follow

Exercise: Strengthen the Character of Your Community

Time to walk your talk, and to reach out to others and invite them to join with you.

What specific behaviors and actions will you regularly demonstrate so as to support these important community values or guiding principles?

See PDF Worksheet p. 55

What specific behaviors and actions will you ask *others* to regularly demonstrate so as to support these important community values or guiding principles?

See PDF Worksheet p. 55

The greatness of a community is most accurately measured by the compassionate actions of its members, a heart of grace, and a soul generated by love."

— Coretta Scott King

The Main Thing Is to Keep the Main Thing the Main Thing!

Consider this bit of wisdom: *The main thing is to keep the main thing the main thing!*

Now let's put it to use: *If the main thing is to keep the main thing the main thing, what's the main thing?*

If the main thing is to keep the main thing the main thing, what are the main principles that will guide your actions?

Answer that riddle, and you will know how to act, in good winds and bad, when the choice is easy and, more important, when the choice is hard.

When you know who you are and who you commit to be, your choice of actions flows more easily and spontaneously, without a need for prolonged deliberation or strategizing or weighing the pros and cons.

Knowing who you are and who you commit to be is a discipline. It will equip you with a set of rules that allow you to engage in any game that your personal and professional lives offer up.

Knowing who you are and who you commit to be is a discipline that is tremendously liberating. The discipline imposed by the rules can free you of the chronic need to weigh, wonder, consider or calculate how to act or how to play, a need that accompanies an absence of rules.

Whatever actions you live by and play by, they become your signature. Now, we all routinely offer our handwritten signature in ways small to large, routine to rare, from signing a credit card slip for coffee to signing a tax return. Yet, much more often, we offer our signature through our actions, ranging from regularly pausing to offer a genuine hello and thank you to the coffeehouse barista to responding honestly in situations where we fear that the truth might be to our disadvantage or detriment. Small or large, pedestrian to profound, your actions *are* your signature.

When I take the time to look closely enough around me, I see plenty of individuals who effortlessly demonstrate character — I say *effortlessly*, because they know who they are to such a degree that they act on principle as a matter of course.

I see them when someone:

- returns too much change given at the register.
- picks up trash left on the beach by someone else.
- takes in a stray dog, tracks down the owner and returns her safely home.
- buys at a locally owned store, even if prices might be slightly higher than at the chain store.

I also see individuals who act from their core when it could be so much more effortless for them to do otherwise.

I see them in the man, woman or young person who take it upon themselves to:

- stand up against bullying — including the bullying of gay and lesbian teenagers.
- stand up against the disrespect and sexual abuse of women.
- advocate on behalf of dignity, equality or fairness.

And, I am heartened when I see or read stories about men, women and young adults who admit to struggling with whether to act on principle or not, and ultimately choose to do so, even when it might be more advantageous for them not to do so.

Consider the following story[3] taken from the local news in Tempe, Arizona, in November 2010.

---

3. Sources: *The Arizona Republic, Associated Press, Huffington Post, USA Today.*

HOMELESS MAN FINDS, TURNS IN BACKPACK WITH $3,300 INSIDE

Dave Talley, a homeless man, found an abandoned backpack at a train station. When he looked inside with the thought of finding the owner's identification or contact information, he found instead a laptop and $3,300 in cash. Talley had lost his home several years before, and had been living in shelters run by the Tempe Community Action Agency (TCAA). Talley admitted that he was tempted to keep the money, but he said his conscience kicked in, and he decided to turn it in. "There's lots of money I could have taken," he said, but "the fact of the matter was it was not my money. I didn't earn it. I could have done a lot of things with the money," he said, "but none of them would've been right. I'm the one that has to lay down every day and deal with myself. If I'd done anything different than what I did, I don't know if I could handle that."

Talley sought the help of the staff at the TCAA and the local police to identify and contact the rightful owner of the backpack and its contents. It was Arizona State University student Bryan Belanger. He said he had unwittingly left the bag behind at the station five days earlier and had not expected to see it or his money again. When he did get it all back, and found that "not a dollar was missing," he said, "this is the greatest thing I've ever experienced, I think. It is really a lesson to keep your faith in people. Character exists no matter what your circumstances."

Now, back to you and to the question: What signature do you want to be known by? What set of principles are you prepared to embrace privately, and share publicly? What is the signature by which you *will* be known?

To that end, take some time to wrap your arms around all your introspection, your reflection, your inquiry and your data from the prior pages. On the next two pages, capture the main principles that are and will be your signature. These are the main things. And, after all, *the main thing is to keep these main things the main thing!*

Exercise: What Signature Do I Want to Be Known By?

PERSONAL VALUES

I am known by these personal guiding principles that I already regularly demonstrate through my actions. (Refer to your notes on pages 79–80.)

See PDF Worksheet p. 56

VALUES I ASPIRE TO

I aspire to be known by these guiding principles and commit to regularly demonstrate them in the future. (Refer to your notes on pages 82–83.)

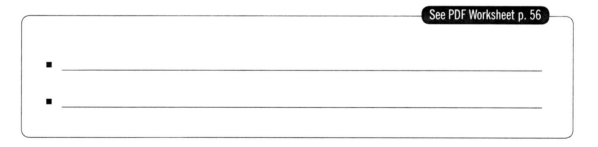

See PDF Worksheet p. 56

VALUES OF MY COMMUNITY

I am and aspire to be known by these community values that I will regularly demonstrate through my actions. (Refer to your notes on pages 108–109, 119.)

See PDF Worksheet p. 57

- _____
- _____
- _____
- _____

These are values we would be well served to adopt in our community. I commit to demonstrate them through my actions. (Refer to your notes on pages 120–121.)

See PDF Worksheet p. 57

- _____
- _____

Life is the raw material.
You are the artist.
Create a thing of beauty."

— Andreas Evriviades
    High-school teacher and coach
    to Peter Alduino

My Character Guides My Actions

You express your character through your actions, behavior, speech and choices. That is the signature through which you become known to your family, friends, community and the world around you. This is the stuff of which a meaningful life is made and credibility is built.

On the illustration that follows, I try to capture the notion that while we have a multitude of possible means and methods (way of acting, speaking and so on) by which we achieve an end, our values can be the filter that ensures that the signature of our character is consistent over time.

Let me recall the words of Ralph Waldo Emerson, who observed, *"As to methods (means) there may be a million and then some, but principles are few. The man who grasps principles can successfully select his own methods. The man who tries methods, ignoring principles, is sure to have trouble."*

Look to the principles on the previous pages that you worked so diligently to discern and define. And look at the illustration on the next page as you promise to yourself:

Whatever ends I am pursuing (or being asked or required to pursue), and whatever hundreds of means there might be for achieving those ends, I will gauge my means — my actions — only after I have run them through the filter of my guiding principles.

This assessment frees me to choose the principle-guided actions that are entirely in keeping with who I am and who I commit to be — in sum, with the signature by which I want to be known.

As I pursue what I want to have or do or experience in my communities and in my life — I am the final arbiter of my actions.

My choice of actions reveals my character. And through my actions, I am revealed.

Principle-Guided Actions

Means and Actions

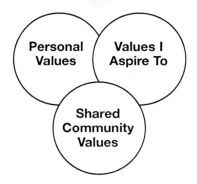

**Means and Actions
That Are Inconsistent
with My Principles**

**Principle-Guided
Means and Actions**

Ⓐ Ⓒ Ⓖ

*I am the
final arbiter
of my actions.*

ENDS

*Seek refuge in yourself. The knowledge of having acted
justly is all your reasoning inner self needs, to be fully
content and at peace with itself."*

— Marcus Aurelius, *Meditations*

The FLIP Side of Leadership . . . and the Antidote

For every leadership development seminar I conduct, I ask each participant to gather some objective data on the topic of leadership ahead of time. Specifically, I ask each person to talk with a few of their friends, family, students, coworkers or acquaintances about leadership in the days before the seminar, and find out what *they* look for in *someone whose lead they would willingly follow*. The operative word here, I stress to my participants, is *"willingly."*[4] *Willingly* means that we exercise our free will. *Willingly* means that we are not coerced, cajoled or backed into a corner to have to follow. Instead, we follow by personal choice, without reluctance, because we are favorably disposed to do so.

More often than not, the soon-to-be participants find, to their surprise, that the people they talk to respond by saying that they look for a similar set of qualities in their own leaders.

---

4. The workshop I refer to here is *The Leadership Challenge Workshop*, created by leadership researchers and writers Jim Kouzes and Barry Posner. When I ask participants, before the workshop, what they "look for in someone whose lead they would willingly follow," and when I go on to stress that the operative word is "willingly," I am conducting an exercise using the "Characteristics of an Admired Leader" questionnaire authored by Kouzes and Posner — an instrument they have been using since 1981 to collect data. For more information on the questionnaire and the data collected, see *The Leadership Challenge* (4th edition), Chapter 2: "Credibility Is the Foundation of Leadership."

Among the qualities they mention most often, *and* what the people say those qualities really mean, are the following:

Honesty . . . is truthful in both word and deed

Integrity . . . walks the talk, consistently

. . . role-models behavior

. . . holds himself or herself accountable

Vision . . . guides, shows the way

. . . communicates objectives and goals

Competence . . . knows the business

Courage . . . adheres to his or her convictions

. . . shows strength of character

Inspires . . . demonstrates personal passion

. . . motivates others

Respects . . . treats others with fairness

. . . remains open to others' ideas

Listens . . . values others' input and ideas

. . . engages in two-way communication

Commits to helping
others succeed . . . strives to know the total person

. . . develops the talent of others

Distributes ownership . . . and holds others accountable

Recognizes and celebrates
others' accomplishments . . . expresses gratitude

. . . gives credit where credit is due, publicly

All of these are admirable qualities. All are typical qualities of exemplary leaders, as cited by scores of prominent practitioners, observers, researchers, writers and teachers in the leadership field. I am confident that, among these, you will find qualities that figure prominently in attracting and engaging your own enthusiasm and commitment to willingly follow the lead of someone else.

Unheralded scores of men and women honor the people they lead by regularly holding themselves accountable for behaving and acting in ways that reflect these qualities. To these people, we owe a debt of gratitude for shaping cultures of ethics, civility and service, as well as for creating great places to work and live.

When my seminar participants ask colleagues about the qualities they value, they seldom report finding *too many* of these qualities in leaders or in their cultures. Far more often, participants report hearing people complain of a scarcity of these qualities among many who don the robes of leader, but who discredit the role by their actions. From my vantage point as one who often hears from those on the receiving end of leadership, their day-to-day experience differs radically from the ideals that they honor or hope for — is far removed, in fact, from the qualities that would engage their enthusiasm to *willingly* follow. In their place, I hear of a bleak set of leadership qualities being practiced by many who call themselves *leader*, but whose actions prove otherwise. Their actions show them to be but pretenders[5] who harm the people they lead by all too frequently choosing to disregard the qualities their people respect and require. Instead, they perpetrate a set of behaviors I've come to call the *FLIP side of leadership.*

FLIP is an inverted (or, worse, distorted) form of leadership whose adherents find it acceptable to:

F — **F**earmonger, **F**abricate claims and **F**alsify the record

L — **L**imit access to information or **L**ie about the facts

I — **I**mpugn the integrity of any detractors and **I**ntimidate them

P — Pursue **P**ower, **P**rofit, **P**restige, **P**osition, **P**ersonal or **P**rofessional Gain, **P**ublicity or **P**leasure, with callous disregard for principle or the interests of the community and the common good

A casual reading of the news and blogs in this first decade of the 21st century offers myriad stories of women and men in every office of leadership — be it in our business communities, religious communities, school systems, or in our national, state and local governments, or in our not-for-profit organizations — whose actions and behaviors illustrate the FLIP side of leadership. Their motivations have more to do with exerting control than with inspiring us to contribute; more to do with getting compliance than with engaging our desire or our willingness to commit; more to do with serving the immediate interests of a few than with the larger

---

5. One who makes a false or hypocritical show.

interests of the community they claim to lead. They might wear the label "leader"; they might hold the title "leader"; but they are *not* leaders. Rather, they are "handlers" posing as leaders. They do little to engage our enthusiasm or inspire us to *willingly* follow. Instead, they too often *manage and manipulate* the people under their cloak to follow out of fear, self-interest or self-preservation.

I have written *The Citizen Leader* partially in response to this practice.

I fundamentally believe that we are all co-creators of the world in which we live and work. Our families, our schools, our places of work, our places of worship, our neighborhoods and towns — all these constitute the communities that make up our world. Through our daily behaviors, words, actions and choices, we contribute to the character of those communities, and shape the world in which we live and work, for ourselves, for our families, for our friends, for our colleagues, for our coworkers and for our fellow citizens.

I fundamentally believe that if we wish to avoid living under the FLIP side of leadership, then we must assume personal responsibility to check it, right it, reverse it. I fundamentally believe that if I myself do little or nothing to arrest this FLIP dynamic, I am condoning both its growth and the culture it produces. I own that while I lack the power to change the world, I do have the power to shape *my* world. And I own that not to take that seriously, not to act as if I am a co-creator of our collective reality, is an act of surrender and perhaps an abdication of responsibility. And so, I try to be mindful of the culture I want to live in as I age, and I try to match my behaviors and actions to that culture.

It's up to us. *We are the ones we are waiting for.* We are the ones who can shape, change and transform our world by behaving and speaking in ways that offer an antidote to the FLIP side of leadership — in ways that will heartily engage the enthusiasm of the people we lead. At the risk of being prescriptive, I offer the following:

Where the handlers would fearmonger, fabricate claims and falsify the record in order to manage and manipulate the people around them, let us **forge a shared understanding of what is real and what is not**.

Where the handlers would limit access to information and lie about the facts, let us **level with one another** so that we may all make clear and informed choices.

Where the handlers would intimidate or impugn the integrity of detractors, let us **inquire into the reasons for disagreement** so that we may **seek to better understand** and **better appreciate differing points of view**.

Where the handlers would pursue power, profit, prestige or personal gain with callous disregard for the deleterious impact on people, community and culture, let us **persevere with adherence to principles that shape a culture of ethics, civility and service**.

It's up to us.

The value of a leader is directly proportional to a leader's values."
— A Golden Rule from the Notre Dame Executive MBA Program

Your Next Steps

In the months ahead, come back and review the readings, the questions, your writings and your responses in this first part of *The Citizen Leader*. Continue your inquiry and exploration. Do not expect to answer the questions once and for all. Instead, hold them in the palm of your hand, and have the curiosity and humility to revisit them time and again to strengthen the substance of your character — who you are, and who you strive to be. Be rigorous. Be honest. Ground yourself, and insist that the content of your character guide your behaviors, your words, your choices and your actions.

Here are several specific ongoing activities and actions for you to pursue:

- Revisit your guiding principles: *What Signature Do I Want to Be Known By?* Look at them regularly. Refine them over time. Let them be an enduring code of conduct to help guide your behaviors, words, choices and actions, both in private and in public.
- Share your personal and public guiding principles with your colleagues and other members of your community. Publicly commit to behave and speak in ways that are in line with them.
- Ask members of your community for feedback from time to time. To collect data, have a face-to-face conversation, or use the *Guiding Principles Dashboard* (pages 222–224). You might find it convenient to use a fill-in PDF version of this dashboard to give or send to others. It is available online for you to complete and download at **www.thecitizenleader.com/worksheets-tcl-1**.

- Engage your colleagues and other members of your community in a dialogue about values for your community. Together, align on standards and expectations for your behaviors, speech, choices and actions that are consistent with those values.
- Periodically reassess the strength of your engagement and adherence to the values of your community. Use the *Community Values Dashboard* (pages 225–227) or the fill-in PDF version available online at **www.thecitizenleader.com/worksheets-tcl-1**.

Be true to your word, your work, and your friend."

— Henry David Thoreau

The Citizen Leader

PART TWO

ACTIVE CITIZEN

It is not the critic who counts; not the man who points out how the strong man stumbles, or where the doer of deeds could have done them better. The credit belongs to the man (or woman) who is actually in the arena, whose face is marred by dust and sweat and blood; who strives valiantly; who errs, and comes short again and again, because there is no effort without error and shortcoming; but who does actually strive to do the deeds; who knows the great enthusiasms, the great devotions; who spends him or herself in a worthy cause; who at the best knows in the end the triumph of high achievement, and who at the worst, if he fails, at least fails while daring greatly, so that his place shall never be with those cold and timid souls who know neither victory nor defeat."

— Theodore Roosevelt, excerpt from the speech "Citizenship In A Republic" delivered at the Sorbonne, in Paris, France, on April 23, 1910

Contribution

Contribution in Service to My Communities

Up to this point, I have been asking you to journey inside, to journey into your hearts and to explore the truth of your convictions and your guiding principles. That has allowed you to get more grounded in *who you are* and to commit to be of such character that you'd want to follow your own lead. Your commitment to character centers on promising *and* acting in ways that clearly reflect the values you espouse. Your commitment to character radiates outward to the world around you as you demonstrate that you are the final arbiter of your actions.

In this second part of *The Citizen Leader* — Active Citizenship — I will guide you as you emerge from the journey inside and apply the energy of your convictions and the qualities of your character to actively make meaningful contributions in your communities. This emphasis toward contribution moves you more fully into the realm of active citizenship. It is your emergence from a place of reflection into a world in which you purposefully apply your heart — and now your head and your hands-on efforts — to improve the lives of other members of your community that shows you to inhabit more fully the role of **active citizen**.

As you apply your qualities of character to actions that will benefit the common good, you are completing the journey from the inside out. Borrowing the words of the renowned American philosopher and master teacher of mythology Joseph Campbell, you are completing *the hero's journey*. Campbell writes that it takes courage, in fact "a hell of a lot of courage,"[6] to continue the journey. Let me echo Campbell by saying it takes courage — at times, a lot of courage — to act as a citizen, to *be* the active citizen.

In the course of the four chapters that follow, I will talk about courage, but I will start with a focus on action and the source of your enthusiasm to take action. That source is love — love for your community and for your place and participation in that community. In Part One of this book, I wrote that the caliber of the actions you take, or indeed even your willingness to take action at all, is directly proportional to your beliefs and feelings about your community. That tenet continues to hold true. So, in this initial chapter of Part Two, I will guide you through a series of questions that will help you reconsider and even deepen your convictions about your community. Your anchor as an active citizen is and will always be in your heart. These questions speak to your heart. As you consider each one, strive to uncover the deeper truth — your deeper truth — about your community and your place in it. Your truth will be the source of your energy and enthusiasm to serve, to act and to persevere.

---

6. Source: *A Joseph Campbell Companion: Reflections on the Art of Living*, p.82

Exercise: Contribution in Service to My Community (for individuals)

[Note: If you're working in a group, please use the version of this exercise designed for group work on page 148.]

Take a closer and deeper look at the community you assessed in the previous section. Write your thoughts on the following:

Who are the people I serve in this community?

See PDF Worksheet p. 59

What do I love about the people I serve?

See PDF Worksheet p. 59

I am deeply grateful to the people I serve for . . .

See PDF Worksheet p. 60

What do I love about the products I offer or the services I perform in this community?

See PDF Worksheet p. 60

How do these products or services enrich the lives of the people I serve?

See PDF Worksheet p. 61

How would the lives or the experience of those people be diminished if I did not exist?

See PDF Worksheet p. 61

What is *my* purpose in my community or my organization?

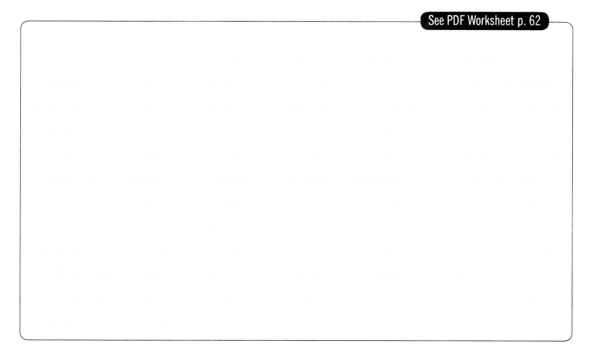

See PDF Worksheet p. 62

On the next page, answer this last question once again, but this time, do it **without** words.

Surrender your thoughts to your creative side. Sketch your thoughts. Doodle, draw, diagram or design your answer to the question: What is *my* purpose in my community or my organization?

Really, let yourself get carried away for just a few moments, or longer. It can be quite revealing. No one is looking. No one is going to grade this exercise.

Use color.

Hold the question both in your head and in your heart, and allow your hands to translate the thoughts that come up into images, symbols, stick figures, squiggles . . .

See PDF Worksheet p. 63

Sketching your thoughts — surrendering and entrusting your thoughts to images or symbols — can be a wonderfully powerful tool to help you develop your own clarity. Here's how.

Look at what you have sketched. Now out loud — and this is key: you can do this alone or with someone else, but out loud — explain what you have drawn. Out loud, explain how your sketch answers this question: What is your purpose in your community or your organization?

As you hear yourself speaking, are *you* clear? Are you candid? Are you convincing (do you believe it)? If not, perhaps some more doodling or drawing is in order — more discovery, more discernment. This exercise is a continuation of your deepening your self-awareness.

Keep at it until what you hear yourself say rings true to you. Keep answering out loud until the sound of what you are saying resonates in your head *and* in your heart.

Now, if you want, you can use words in the space below to capture your deeper, more candid and more resonant answer to the question:

What is *my* purpose in my community or my organization?

See PDF Worksheet p. 64

Exercise: Contribution in Service to Our Community (for groups)

[*Note: If you're doing this exercise as an individual, please use the version of this exercise designed for individual work on page 142.*]

You might be working through your role as an active citizen alongside other members of your team or community. If so, you might find it helpful to consider the questions on the previous few pages with the mind-set that you *and others* are making a *contribution in service to your communities*.

Below you will find the questions tailored for you to answer as a member of a larger group.

Who are the people we serve?

See PDF Worksheet p. 65

What do I love about the people we collectively serve?

See PDF Worksheet p. 65

I am deeply grateful to the people we serve for . . .

See PDF Worksheet p. 66

What do I love about the products we offer or the services we perform?

See PDF Worksheet p. 66

How do our products or services enrich the lives of the people we serve?

See PDF Worksheet p. 67

How would the lives or the experience of those people be diminished if we did not exist?

See PDF Worksheet p. 67

What is *our* purpose as an organization?

See PDF Worksheet p. 68

On the next page, answer this last question once again, but this time, do it **without** words.

Surrender your thoughts to your creative side. Sketch your thoughts. Doodle, draw, diagram or design your answer to the question.

Really, let yourself get carried away for just a few moments, or longer. It can be quite revealing. No one is looking. No one is going to grade this exercise.

Use color.

Hold the question both in your head and your heart. Allow your hands to translate.

What is *our* purpose as an organization?

See PDF Worksheet p. 69

In addition to helping you develop clarity of thought, the images and symbols you created will help you share those thoughts with others. While most words dissolve quickly into the deluge of daily chatter, images and symbols endure. So, take advantage of the power that they hold.

When you illustrate your thoughts with images, it is not enough merely to keep a picture in mind. It helps to be able to explain what the picture means, *and* how it relates to your real world — your current world. This is why it is so important for whatever image or symbol you develop to have meaning for you, to resonate with you. Only when you understand it deeply can you share its essence with others in a way that leaves them with an enduring impression.

The benefit to you and to the people around you is that *in the future* the symbol, when reintroduced or resurrected, having initially been well explained and understood, helps others to retrieve the thoughts and the meaning that you worked so hard to formulate.

Now, if you want, with the benefit of your doodles and drawings, you can use words again in the space below to elaborate on your response to:

What is *our* purpose as an organization?

See PDF Worksheet p. 70

6

Active Citizenship

Know . . . Care . . . Act

To act purposefully on behalf of the betterment of other members of one's community is the meaning of active citizenship.

An active citizen is someone who understands their own values, who they aspire to be, what communities they serve and why they care about the members of those communities.

An active citizen strives to make a contribution to their communities, always acting in accordance with their core values.

Active citizenship is composed of three elements:

- You **know** what it is you want to contribute or change.
- You **care** genuinely about the change and the members of the community whose lives the change will affect.
- And you **act** with courage and conviction, especially in the face of obstacles, to make those changes happen.

I used the themes of **know**, **care** and **act** as a diagnostic tool in the *Community Values Dashboard* in the previous chapter. You will find the themes recurring throughout *The Citizen Leader in Action* series. They will help you assess the strength of your own personal engagement with and adherence to your values — in essence, a measure of your integrity — before you attempt to engage the enthusiasm of anyone else to follow your lead.

Know . . . Care . . . Act — it is a framework that will serve you well in preparation for active citizenship, and a prerequisite for your many roles as an engaging leader.

Know . . . Care . . . Act requires you to be truthful with yourself in response to:

- Do I clearly **know** what I am talking about, what I am proposing, what I am asking others to do? Can I clearly explain what is in my **head** to someone else?
- Do I **care** about what I am proposing? Why do I care? And can I express why I care — the feelings in my **heart** — to someone else?
- Do I **act** in ways that demonstrate my commitment to what I know and what I care about? What am I doing now and what will I do in the future to be **hands on?**

So, let's make this real. On these next few pages, I invite you to step vigorously into your role as an active citizen, and draw on the Know . . . Care . . . Act framework to help you champion[7] an initiative or change that you think is important in your community.

I trust that as you apply the framework, you will find it understandable, meaningful and actionable. The questions of the framework prompt you to engage both your head and your heart in any endeavor, and in so doing commit to engage in impactful hands-on actions.

Looking to the future and to the enduring usefulness of *The Citizen Leader* in your life, I hope that you will draw on the Know . . . Care . . . Act framework again and again when, as an active citizen, you seek to participate in and lead initiatives that will improve the lives of others.

---

7. **To champion**: *vt* : to defend, support, promote or fight for a cause or person

Exercise: Know

What initiative or change do I want to champion or am I being asked to lead in my community?

See PDF Worksheet p. 72

What is one piece of evidence that convinces me of the need for the initiative or change?

See PDF Worksheet p. 72

The Citizen Leader: Be the Person You'd Want to Follow

What do I anticipate the key obstacles will be to implementing the initiative or change?

See PDF Worksheet p. 73

What will be the benefits when the initiative or change is successfully implemented?

See PDF Worksheet p. 73

What would be the consequences if it were not implemented?

See PDF Worksheet p. 74

The Citizen Leader: Be the Person You'd Want to Follow

Care

*"Do I **care** about what I am proposing?"*

"Why do I care?"

*"Can I express why I care — the feelings in my **heart** — to someone else?"*

These questions invite you to go deeper and deeper as you reach for your response. This process of going deeper prompts you to take a trip from the head to the heart — to turn an initial response that could look and sound and feel logical into an expression that looks and sounds and feels alive. And it is alive because it is inspired.

Inspire literally means *to breathe life into*. So, I am asking you to reach for an expression of *why you care* that breathes life into you — a prerequisite for your being able to breathe life into anyone else who may want to follow your lead, to want to serve, act or persevere.

Move on from what's logical and let yourself go deeper, and then go deeper still to a place of love — love for the people you lead, love for the people you serve, love for the people of your community. And let that love inspire how you complete, for yourself and to others, this statement: *I personally care about this initiative or change because . . .*

This is what it can look like:

> In the mid-1990s, I was asked by Roger O. to help him plan for a meeting with his staff, at which he wanted to announce a reorganization. He had twelve direct reports, and wanted to reduce that number to only three. The remaining nine people would report up through

those primary three. He knew the reorganization would be unpopular because all twelve were equally competent and equally accomplished individuals. He knew that he would be ruffling the feathers of the nine who would no longer have a direct reporting access or relationship to him. Sound like dry stuff? Here is the not-so-dry part of the story.

Roger was the head of the group of twelve scientists at a company that was developing the key technology for the mapping of the human genome. His scientists were among the best in their field, worldwide.

Roger was convinced that the reorganization was essential to his, and their, being able to accelerate the pace of their work. Speed was of the essence. They were in a race against a European government–funded consortium to develop the technology that would, as clichéd as it sounds, change the world. To the winner would go the spoils.

Roger knew what he wanted to do. That was clear.

I asked him why he cared. Our conversation went like this:

Roger, why do you want to do this? I asked.

This way, I won't have to be the one to review the progress of each person's work, he said.

What else? I asked.

It frees up my time to garner the resources that we need to do our work, he replied.

See, very dry stuff on the surface. Yet the challenge for Roger was to express what was in his heart — what inspired him to want to make the change — what engaged his own enthusiasm. This would be, as I have said, a prerequisite if he was to have any possibility of engaging the enthusiasm of his fellow scientists to participate in the change. Our conversation continued.

Roger, go deeper. Why do you care?

I care about our being successful and beating out our competitors to develop the technology first.

Again, why do you care? I asked.

Peter, this is getting old. I care because our jobs are on the line.

Go deeper. Why is this change personally important to you?

Now ticked off at what seemed like my badgering, Roger slammed his hand on the table that separated our chairs and shouted:

I'll tell you why I care. Five hundred years from now, this time in human history will be remembered for two things: we will have developed the technology to destroy the human race, and we will have developed the technology to save the human race. I want us to be part of developing the technology to save the human race. That's why I care.

If you can reach deep into your heart to discern a depth of caring that stirs up your own feelings and passions, then, like Roger,[8] you will tap into a source of energy that can inspire and sustain you. Then you will tap into a source of energy that can help you build and strengthen your bonds with the people you lead. Then you will tap into a source of energy that can inspire and sustain the people on whose enthusiasm you will rely to participate, to serve, to act and to persevere as you labor together to make a meaningful contribution to your community and to your world.

Your capacity to know and to express *why you care* is a recurring theme in each one of the roles that you will step into as a leader — a prerequisite to your building bonds as an engaging, effective and powerful leader.

---

8. Note: With my permission, this story has been borrowed and fictionalized in the best-selling book *The Radical Leap* by Steve Farber. I am delighted, here, to recognize the original player and share his story with you.

Exercise: Care

I *personally* care about this initiative or change because . . .

See PDF Worksheet p. 75

Go deep:

I *personally* care about this initiative or change because . . .

See PDF Worksheet p. 75

Go deeper:

I *personally* care about this initiative or change because . . .

See PDF Worksheet p. 76

What lies behind us and what lies ahead of us are tiny matters compared to what lies within us."

— Henry David Thoreau

Exercise: Act

At this juncture, you have used the Know . . . Care . . . Act framework to sharpen your understanding (head) of the reasons for the change or initiative you want to lead, and you have probed the deeper reasons for why you personally care (heart). It remains, then, for you to focus on what you are doing now and what you will do in the future to move your initiative forward (hands on!). With a solid foundation of head and heart — with the two forces of understanding and caring solidly in play — you have done the internal work to now act in ways that demonstrate your commitment to your initiative.

Let's get to it:

What are you doing *now* to champion the initiative?

See PDF Worksheet p. 77

Is it having an impact?

See PDF Worksheet p. 77

Impact. It's one of those words that get thrown around without much consideration for what it really means. *And*, it means different things to different people. So, in the interest of bringing rigor to your response, let me pause to give *impact* a working definition. An action has impact, or is impactful, when it has a *compelling effect* — when it *accelerates or shifts the trajectory of the matter at hand in a way that is important or significant.*

So, let's return to the question above: Are your actions having an impact on the initiative?

See PDF Worksheet p. 77

Why do you say so? What are the compelling effects?

See PDF Worksheet p. 77

Now, let's look to the future. Shift your attention to what you could do from this point forward. You have just stated what you are currently doing. Now, imagine and describe other actions you might take that could have a compelling effect on advancing your initiative. As you do so, keep your thinking broad so that you include actions that might engender risk or even fear on your part.

Let me be clear: I am not asking you to consider risk without forethought or evidence of the potential, significant benefit. Indeed, taking risky action without considering what happens next is reckless. And, taking a risk just for the sake of taking a risk is little more than chasing an adrenaline rush.

So, instead, hone your focus to the possible actions that could accelerate or shift the trajectory of your initiative. Write them down, and as you do so, include any and all that you might be afraid to follow through with, *at least for the moment*. This is just the first iteration of this exercise devoted to Act. You are not making any commitments, yet. In the next chapter, you will examine a new way of looking at *courage* to help overcome your fears. With the benefit of that examination, you will revisit the actions you describe here, and then you can decide which ones you will commit to follow through with.

What are possible impactful actions or risks you could take to champion or lead this initiative or change?

See PDF Worksheet p. 78

What are possible impactful actions or risks you could take to address the key obstacles?

See PDF Worksheet p. 78

I know of no more encouraging fact than the unquestionable ability of a man to elevate his life by a conscious endeavor."

— Henry David Thoreau

CHAPTER

Courage

Point of Credibility

I talked at length earlier in this book about the concept of credibility in connection with the promises you make to yourself and others about how you will conduct yourself in the world — about your values and guiding principles. I wrote that when your behaviors, words and choices don't match your promises, you cause others to question your credibility. *And* if the mismatch between your promises and your actual performance persists, you eventually give those around you reason to say to themselves: *I do not believe.*

Here, I'd like to expand on that concept of credibility to also include the actions you take as you attempt to advance your initiative. Consider this: as you choose to champion an initiative or cause, the people around you are gauging your personal credibility both by looking at your behaviors, words and choices *and* by looking to see whether you strive in earnest to advance your initiative by taking the kinds of actions whose potential impact matches the strength of your professed enthusiasm for the cause. It is only when your actions have at least a potential that is proportionate to the passion you profess that you give others reason to believe you care as much as you say you do. Now, it's entirely possible that your actions might not have as strong an impact as you intend. They might fall short for any number of reasons, and at times they will. But the important point here is that your actions need to have a potential that matches your professed enthusiasm if you hope to demonstrate your believability in the eyes of anyone who might be watching. Let me illustrate on the graphic that follows. The diagonal line represents the points at which the potential impact of your actions is directly proportional to the strength of your enthusiasm. I call any point along this line a *point of credibility*. At any of these points where enthusiasm and potential impact of action intersect, you safeguard and even strengthen your credibility in the eyes of those looking to see if you are someone whose lead they would want to follow.

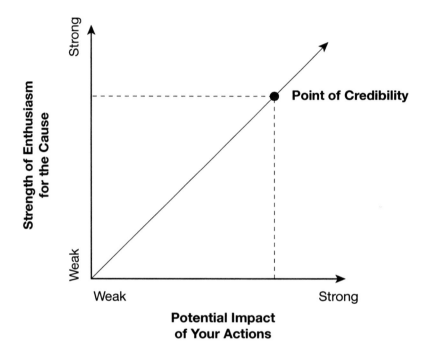

In all probability, there will be times when your enthusiasm for the initiative or cause will be strong, but your fears or the risks will keep you from taking the actions that could have a strong impact on moving it forward (see graphic that follows). That is not to say that you won't take any action at all. To the contrary, often, if not most times, you will. But the question is whether you will take actions that match the strength of your enthusiasm, or whether your fears will temper your actions despite your enthusiasm. When the potential impact of the actions you do take is (or even appears to be) weaker than the care you profess to harbor for the cause, you give others reason to question whether you are indeed committed. And much to your detriment, if you repeatedly resort to timid action, others will have reason to question your credibility.

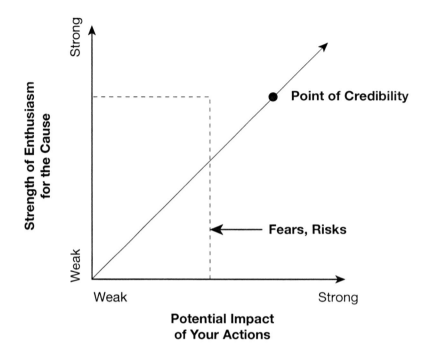

Force of Courage

I ended the previous chapter by guiding you through several questions to help you think broadly about the possible actions you could take. In particular, I challenged you to include impactful actions that might engender risk or fear on your part. Now, let me begin to offer my thoughts about what you can do when your way forward seems blocked. These are the moments to harness the forces that will allow you to push against the fears that are holding you back. These are the moments to garner the forces that will help you to take the actions that *can* have a strong impact on the outcome, and thereby will help you demonstrate your commitment to the cause as well as your credibility in it. Those forces come from the inside. They are housed in the head and in the heart and emerge as a power that allows you to engage in efforts to advance your initiative and, by extension, to make a difference in your community and in your world. Your forceful ally in these efforts to take on the risks that will accelerate or shift the trajectory of your initiative is the *force of courage*.

If we look to the dictionary for a definition of *courage*, we find:

Courage *n* : 1. mental and moral strength to venture, persevere and withstand danger, fear or difficulty; 2. firmness of mind in the face of danger or extreme difficulty

So, at its core, we can say that *courage* is a *resolve of the mind*.
And, there's more.
At the root of the word *courage* is the French word *coeur*, which means *heart*. At its core, then, *courage* is also rooted in the heart. That is to say, we garner our courage, in part, because we care, and that caring helps us generate the force to take on

risk and confront fear — in short, to act! When we take into account both meanings, the full dimension of *courage* reaches broadly to embrace both our mental resolve (head) *and* our caring (heart). It was in anticipation of your needing to garner courage that I asked you, in the previous chapter, to *go deep and even deeper* as you considered why you *personally* care about the initiative or change you want to champion.

Courage, in sum, is the force that allows us to draw on the strength of our mental resolve and our deeper, heartfelt caring to push against fear, and dare to take actions that could have a strong impact as we attempt to advance our initiative or change.

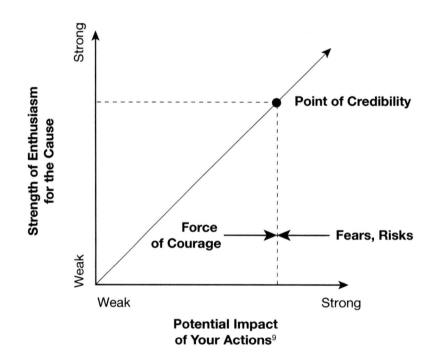

A word of reminder about those actions: you spent considerable time in Part One of *The Citizen Leader* reflecting on and refining the qualities of the person you are and aspire to be. You committed to the signature by which you want to be known in the world (even when no one else is looking). That signature — consisting of your values and guiding principles — is on display when you take

---

9. Principle-guided actions: In keeping with your values and guiding principles

on the risks and confront your fears. As you know clearly from your work in Part One, by choosing to act in ways that are consistent with your values and guiding principles, you safeguard your personal integrity and you protect your credibility in the minds and eyes of others. As we go forward in this chapter, I am assuming that you will continue to commit to behave, speak and make choices in ways that are *principle guided*.

Fears and Risks

The fears and risks that hold us back take on many forms — fear of or risk of failure, of forfeit, of consequence, of loss . . .

I'd like to consider one particular set of fears and risks that I find cause much anguish, yet present themselves at some point in the lives of most all of us. That set of fears and risks concerns our falling out of favor with family, friends, loved ones and colleagues.

As human beings, we all harbor and act on a set of five fundamental, life-sustaining needs. These needs, first articulated and described by the renowned American psychologist Abraham Maslow in his *hierarchy of five human needs*, form the cornerstone of what is modern humanistic psychology.

Maslow's Hierarchy of Needs

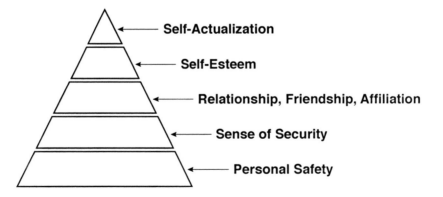

At the foundation of the hierarchy, Maslow identifies two needs that are necessary for our survival as human beings: our need for personal safety and our need for a sense of security. I touch here on Maslow's hierarchy and point out his notion of *survival needs*, which will help you understand why, when you are uncertain of the outcome of your actions (however meritorious or principle guided they might be), you might choose **not** to act. Why do you? Because of:

- fear that your personal safety might be threatened, or
- fear that the substance of your personal security might be taken away: income, job, position, title, perks, benefits packages, your health care, your home . . .

But, if you *do* choose to act:

- Privately, if you know what is on the line when you are faced with the choice of whether or not to act on behalf of a cause that you care about, then your deliberate choice to take action is evidence of the strength of your enthusiasm.
- Publicly, if you profess to care strongly about a cause, and you consciously choose to act in the face of fear and risk in support of that cause, you demonstrate the credibility that allows others to know you care. You demonstrate the credibility that lets those whose efforts you might need to enlist see your courage in action.

The gains that you earn when you tap into the force of your courage and take strong action are those of feeding your human hunger for self-esteem (feeling good about yourself) and self-actualization (believing that you are living up to your full potential). Maslow identifies both of these as *psychological needs* that are necessary to our well-being. But, he also tells us that it is only after we have satisfied our survival needs that we can, or do, lend our attention and efforts to feeding our hunger for psychological health and fulfillment.

Sandwiched in between survival needs and psychological needs, Maslow places the human need for relationship, friendship and affiliation. In brief, he reminds us that we require human bonding. It is an essential need both for our survival and for our psychological well-being. Our bonds with others support us; they sustain us; they are a source of family and camaraderie and collegiality. They answer our yearning for connection and company. They give us a sense of place and belonging.

And yet, there are those who would wield those bonds to subjugate us or, worse, to sabotage us — sometimes wittingly, but often not. Sometimes a family member or a friend or a work colleague might condition their continued favor on our conforming to their expectations or requirements. So I ask you to pay heed. When a requirement to conform starts to become a ceiling limiting your growth (whether mental, moral, emotional or spiritual), you become a servant. The bonds become shackles. Consider this alternative: when you choose to act as you deem fit, rather than as another might deem fit, even if to do so puts your bond with them at risk, your action is not a risk at all. Instead, when you garner the courage to speak up and act as *you* deem fit, you access a higher need — the need for personal self-esteem. Yes, you might jeopardize bonds that have been made conditional on your speaking or acting in ways that meet someone else's imperatives, but, more importantly, you safeguard your own. Ultimately, the true nature of your friendships and affiliations will be revealed, and you will better know the bonds that truly nourish.

It takes courage to act in defiance of the possibility that your actions might cause you to fall out of favor with friends, family, coworkers or members of your community. Yet, when you take those actions to safeguard your principles, you strengthen your integrity, secure your credibility and honor your true self.

Now, let's focus on what you will do — even (or especially) under the pressures and duress of fear and risk.

First, do you think you have the necessary *force of courage* to champion the initiative or change that you think is important in your community?

See PDF Worksheet p. 80

Why? or Why Not?

See PDF Worksheet p. 80

Second, there is nothing that says you need to be taking on the initiative or change without the support of others in your community or in your world. So, if you feel that you lack the necessary *force of courage*, whose support could you enlist to help you overcome your reservations and fears? And what will you ask of each of these individuals?

See PDF Worksheet p. 81

Finally, use the word *courage* as a verb. Yes, you read that correctly. Use it as an action verb to commit to the actions that you will take to advance the initiative or the change you personally care about.

You identified several possible paths of action on pages 166–167 to champion your cause and move beyond key obstacles. Now, gather your courage — your mental resolve and your heart — to commit to act. Express, in writing, your resolve to confront the risk or fear that is holding you back or that might have done so in the past. Express your courage with these words:

I courage to . . .

Exercise: I *Courage* to . . .

What *impactful* principle-guided actions do *I courage* to take *in the next three weeks to* champion or lead this initiative or change?

Action: I *courage* to . . .

See PDF Worksheet p. 82

Why *this* action?

See PDF Worksheet p. 82

What will be the measure of progress?

> See PDF Worksheet p. 82

Action: **I *courage* to . . .**

> See PDF Worksheet p. 83

Why *this* action?

> See PDF Worksheet p. 83

What will be the measure of progress?

> See PDF Worksheet p. 83

Action: **I _courage_ to . . .**

See PDF Worksheet p. 84

Why _this_ action?

See PDF Worksheet p. 84

What will be the measure of progress?

See PDF Worksheet p. 84

Broaden ... Rediscover ... Reconnect

At times the nature of our activities, for any number of reasons, diminishes our passions for the cause or the purpose of our work. And at times, despite our actions (effective though we might be), our enthusiasm weakens and wanes.

At other times, routine, repetition and rote behavior tend to narrow our field of play so that we see only what is directly in front of us. We can get so mired in the daily minutiae that our view of what we are doing, and why, becomes myopic. We see the morass around us, not the blue sky above. While initially it might be a place of predictability and comfort, that chronic confined focus is apt to devolve into a detached compliance or disheartening capitulation.

What can we do?

We can take three steps to move out of our mire and myopia. We can:

- *broaden the focus of our work* in such a way that allows us to . . .
- *rediscover the purpose and meaning in our daily activities*, and . . .
- *reconnect at a heartfelt level with the cause and with our selves*.

The good news is that you have already done the necessary introspective work to navigate your way through these three steps. You just need to remind yourself. In Chapter 5, you gave considerable thought to both the love you have for your community and your place and purpose in that community. Your looking back at that good work will provide you with a source of ideas (head) and feelings (heart) to help you broaden your focus, rediscover your purpose and reconnect with the cause that has energized you in the past.

Exercise: Broaden . . . Rediscover . . . Reconnect

Let me guide you as you look back and reconnect with the sources of your enthusiasm.

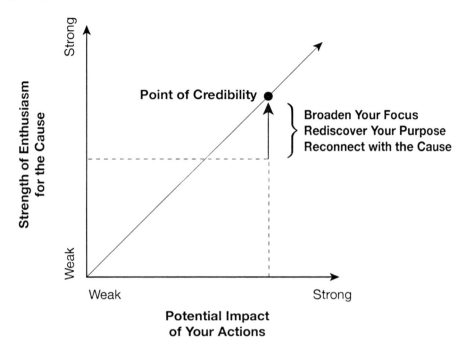

BROADEN YOUR FOCUS

Call back to heart and mind your convictions about the people you serve, and how the services or products you provide enrich their lives (pages 142–144, 148–149).

As you take the time to look back and remind yourself what you love about these people and see how your services or products enrich their lives, what broader perspective comes into focus about your current endeavors?

See PDF Worksheet p. 85

REDISCOVER YOUR PURPOSE

Remember the purpose of your daily activities — the *purpose* that has *breathed life into you* in the past. Remind yourself how your purpose infused your daily activities with meaning, and how it inspired you to be an active citizen and to contribute to your community (pages 145–147).

I know you have written this down before; you've even drawn it out. Yet, for your own encouragement — to give yourself a shot of mental resolve and heartfelt caring at a time when your enthusiasm might be waning — jot down once again your thoughts to the question: What is *my* purpose in my community or my organization?

See PDF Worksheet p. 85

How do your daily activities help you fulfill your purpose?

See PDF Worksheet p. 86

RECONNECT WITH THE CAUSE

Finally, remember that the nature of your work might be an integral part of a larger whole, a larger pursuit. Bring that to mind once again. Recall the contribution that your group or organization makes to the lives of all the citizens of the community (pages 150–152).

What is that contribution?

How does your group or organization's contribution better the lives of others?

See PDF Worksheet p. 86

Force of Courage to Redirect or Reinvent

What happens when, with introspection and reflection, we realize that we are acting on behalf of a cause for which we have little passion and have lost our enthusiasm? The operative words here are *little* and *lost*. It is normal for almost all of us to spend *some time* taking care of the routine, the mundane and even sometimes the distasteful — all of which might cause our enthusiasm to wane. But what happens when, despite our best efforts to be and stay engaged, we find that *some time* becomes *too much of the time*? When taking care of the matters at hand makes us reluctant, resistant, even resentful? What can we do when our spirit, our sense of self, suffers because the cause no longer gives us much enthusiasm or strength to carry on?

We can garner the force of our courage to redirect our efforts or to reinvent ourselves.

Redirect

We can redirect our talents to make a meaningful contribution to another cause that we *do* care about strongly. Metaphorically, if the table at which we currently dine no longer nourishes our spirits — or, worse, depletes us — we can change tables, switch venues. This is an act of courage. This is an act of mental resolve and caring, an act of love, both for ourselves *and* for the people closest to us.

Whenever we *courage* to take steps to nourish our spirits — in this case, by redirecting our talents and our efforts to a more meaningful cause — we engage our own enthusiasm, which is the prerequisite to our engaging the enthusiasm of the other people in our lives and in our community.

There have been many times over the course of my life and career when I've redirected my efforts. Let me illustrate with a few.

Twelve years ago, I redirected my efforts when I resigned my job with a prestigious training and consulting company to form my own practice, Bridge Group Communications. My motivation, as you might recall from my earlier story when I talked about values, was to revive my spirits and restore my enthusiasm for the work I loved (but had grown to resent).

During the prior eight years, I had traveled throughout the country and the world to consult with and conduct professional development seminars for executives and management teams. It was stimulating work that drew on a wide range of my talents, experience and expertise. It was emotionally demanding work that required me to tune into and respond to a great variety of personalities and personal agendas. And it was isolating work that found me eating alone, sleeping in luxurious but lonely hotel rooms and returning to my rented apartment in San Francisco for only a few days a week (if that). It was difficult to deepen friendships or form a primary relationship. In the last couple of years, my spirits sank with every new request to take on a new assignment or client. My enthusiasm took a nosedive. And worst of all, so did my professional performance.

No one was at fault. It was just that the travel requirements of the job, despite the rewards they offered, no longer provided the sustenance I needed to be a whole and healthy human being. I lingered for a while, holding onto security, hoping that I could learn to live life in between my assignments away. But candidly, I was afraid to let go.

And then I did. In a moment when I was faced with the prospect of nine weeks of back-to-back assignments on the road (with only the weekends at home), I acted with resolve (head) and with love for my spirit (heart) to step away — to resign my position and to forge a different path in the world to which I could apply my professional talents.

And it was hard.

Yet I am grateful that I garnered the courage to do it.

Fire a Boss, Find a Leader

I have found that while I enjoyed the food and friendship of others at my own metaphorical table, I had great difficulty with the person sitting at the head: the boss. One of my bosses, in particular, was an unapologetic bully.

I recall being jazzed by my work and enjoying the camaraderie and smarts of my colleagues. I really did not want to change jobs or to abandon the people we served, not to mention the members of our broader community. Yet my spirits were being sucked dry by the dysfunction of an individual, my boss, who went about bullying her staff. She did this by telling us what to do and often how to do it — meaning, her way — *and* she rationalized her behavior because, as she reminded us at staff meetings, *"Your job is to help me make my bonus."*

It was not the work that failed to nourish my spirits. It was the failure of the boss.

Hoping that the situation would improve and also perhaps feeling afraid to leave my job, I continued to tolerate this boss's bad behavior, probably for too long. The environment was toxic, and I reached a point at which I felt toxic too — by which I mean, I felt an internal cynicism for the work and the workplace. Even worse, I found that my sour spirits tainted my life outside of work, too. Not a good way of being or living at the age of 35, or at any age!

I did eventually leave. I did eventually garner the force of courage to resign from that job, and sought to redirect my skills and efforts elsewhere.

It was hard.

I didn't have a secure position to move on to.

Yet, with hindsight, I can say that *couraging* to leave that toxic environment and boss revived my spirits and opened the doors to possibilities that I could never have imagined or scripted for myself.

I subsequently partnered up with a leader who operated from a place of love — love for the work *and* love for the talented people under his tutelage who devoted their energies to doing the work. I credit this leader for my deliberate use of the words *partnered up*, for, while he was the leader, he purposefully acted in ways that promoted partnership with everyone who worked for him. It was he who introduced me to the realm of leadership, both as a profession and, more importantly, as a daily practice.

Reinvent

Finally, at certain points in our lives we might reach a fork in the road where we need, or want or are called on (by external events, a shift in conscience, a bolt of inspiration), to reinvent ourselves — points at which we are better served to stop what we are doing, altogether; graciously bow out; leave; and then apply ourselves and our talents to an endeavor that is entirely different.

In particular, consider the significant transitions in our life that present us with the opportunity, if not the obligation, to reinvent ourselves. Among those are times:

- When we go from dependent to independent
- When we go from school to job
- When we go from single to partnered, and vice versa
- When we go from being childfree to being a parent, and then to an empty-nester
- When we go from working to not working
- When we go from healthy to debilitated
- If we go from private figure to public figure, and then back
- If we go from subordinate to boss, and then back
- If we go from vibrant to infirm

Additionally, consider the times when we may, or must, courageously and consciously *choose* to take the fork that leads away from life as we know it, and reinvent ourselves — times that ask us to choose and to change and to reinvent ourselves, out of love for ourselves and, by extension, out of love for the people around us.

Let me illustrate with the story of a young man I met on a plane going to the Midwest several years ago. Seated next to one another, we talked about our professions. His was one that was brand new to me. He spent his days visiting independent farmers, enlisting their interest in and commitment to incorporating wildlife conservation practices into their farming. In particular, he worked with them to figure out ways to cultivate their land while protecting the natural bird-habitats that were there.

As we chatted, I asked him about the route he had traveled to get to this kind of work. It turned out that it lay along a fork in the road that had taken him far afield of his original career trajectory. Several years earlier, he was one semester from graduating from college with a bachelor's degree in business when his father died unexpectedly. The young man told me that in the weeks after the funeral, as he reflected on his own place in life, he came to admit to himself that the pursuit of a career in business was not what *he* wanted to do. It was, it turns out, what his *father* had wanted him to do. And he had been going through the motions to please him.

So with one semester to go, and only himself to answer to, he stopped altogether, dropped out of the business program and started over in a field for which he truly had a passion — environmental conservation. When I asked about the passion that had given him the courage to reinvent himself, he answered, "I wanted to protect the wildlife for my children." But he hadn't been married when he took that fork in the road. At the time we talked on the plane, he had a wife and a small daughter.

He loved his work, and I certainly felt that he loved the life he had *couraged* to choose.

I'm with him. I firmly believe that if you find that your current endeavor no longer nourishes your passions or enthusiasm, then, with resolve and love, head and heart, knowing and caring, you can act courageously and launch yourself in a new direction. I firmly believe that when we garner the courage to redirect our efforts or reinvent ourselves, we reclaim ourselves and renew our spirits. We enrich our lives and the lives of the people around us — especially those most dear.

There is a time in every man's education when he arrives at the conviction that envy is ignorance; that imitation is suicide; that he must take himself for better or for worse as his portion; that though the wide universe is full of good, no kernel of nourishing corn can come to him but through his toil bestowed on that plot of ground which is given to him to till. The power which resides in him is new in nature, and none but he knows what that is which he can do, nor does he know until he has tried."

— Ralph Waldo Emerson

Encourage

Hearten Others

You give heart to others . . . when you encourage them.

No act of inviting others to struggle against obstacles and draw on their own courage can possibly sustain itself if the heart grows weak. We as citizen leaders can fuel the hearts of others through our encouragement and gratitude.

When we offer encouragement to others, we extend our hearts to their hearts. Encouragement is the breath that stokes the embers of resolve and love. It ignites and fuels the force of courage for others to carry forward and carry on.

Citizen leadership is for those who willingly extend their hearts to the people they work alongside and lead — and who do so not because they have to but because they *want* to and because they *care*. At its heart, citizen leadership is for those who love.

M. Scott Peck writes insightfully in his best-selling book *The Road Less Traveled*, *"I define love thus: The will to extend one's self for the purpose of nurturing one's own or another's spiritual growth."*

Whether it's where we live or where we work — at home, in school, in our place of work or of worship, our neighborhood or town, our troop or our support group — we have the opportunity to build bonds and engage the enthusiasm of our family, our friends, our colleagues, our coworkers and our fellow citizens, simply by extending our love to them, and by nurturing their spirits with our words of encouragement. We build and strengthen the bonds that move others to enthusiastically engage, serve, act and persevere when we operate from a place of the heart — from a place of love.

You show your love to others . . . when you express your gratitude.

There was a time when I trained rigorously for triathlons — an individual sports race that required me to swim, cycle and run, with each event immediately following the other. Too much of the time during my training, I found myself chronically tired and suffering from low energy. Fortunately, I met a trainer who, with just a few words, made me understand why. His words to me were: "A nickel's worth of gas is only going to get you a nickel's worth of distance." Sounded pretty simple. I just wasn't eating enough. I needed to put more fuel in the tank, *regularly*, if I was going to be able to garner the strength and stamina to endure the rigors of the training and then to compete.

Drawing on my lesson from this experience, I suggest that you will be well served to regularly top off the tanks of your crew members who find themselves needing to gather strength to endure the rigors of the service and work that they perform. And you will be well served to express your gratitude to others *regularly* for their efforts.

Of course, it is reasonable to expect that individuals can and will fuel their own efforts. Nevertheless, your adding your own expression of encouragement will nourish their spirits. It will affirm that you care about the people you lead. Oh, and one more thing: it just might nourish your own spirits as well!

Let's look to your own experience for some proof positive.

Exercise: Gratitude (I)

Gratitude means *a feeling of being thankful to someone for something*.

On the *giving* end:

Recall an occasion when you offered a *meaningful* expression of gratitude to someone.

Specifically, what occurred, and what did you say?

See PDF Worksheet p. 88

What was the impact on *you*?

See PDF Worksheet p. 88

Now, let's take a look at the *receiving* end:

Recall an occasion when you received a *meaningful* expression of gratitude.

Specifically, what occurred; what was said to you — what made it *meaningful?*

See PDF Worksheet p. 89

What was the impact on you?

See PDF Worksheet p. 89

If it was work related, what was the impact on your work?

See PDF Worksheet p. 90

You'll notice that I stressed the word *meaningful* as I talked about gratitude. *Meaningful* lives in the heart. It is a reflection of what is in our heart. And so, a *meaningful* expression of gratitude is one that is heartfelt — felt in the core of both the receiver and *you*.

So, back to the heart — *your* heart. The key to expressing gratitude that has meaning to someone else is first to know and feel that it has meaning for you. Then, by expressing your *heartfelt* gratitude, as with encouragement, you allow for the possibility that it will be felt in the heart of the individual to whom it is offered.

This is very different from throw-away or perfunctory phrases that you might utter to others — such as "thank you!" or "at-a-boy!" or "good job!" — which come from the head. At best, these conventional accolades have people guessing about what you really mean, or why you said them. At worst, they ring hollow and, as a result, carry little meaning for your listener or for you. Metaphorically, you risk serving up a helping of empty carbs with little to no nutritional value. This is not the kind of diet that will provide anything but a nickel's worth of fuel, if that, for the challenges ahead.

So, let's go back to the heart. Allow the following questions to guide you in expressing meaningful gratitude, and by extension in building and strengthening your bonds with the people you lead. Answer them out loud, and pay attention to the feelings that you experience along the way.

What are you thankful for?

Gratitude is not only the greatest of virtues, but the parent of all others."

— Cicero

For what do you feel grateful?

Be specific.

Why are you thankful? Why do you feel grateful?

Go deep. Get clear.

Your capacity to articulate *"why?"* derives from your knowing in your heart why you care!

If your response sounds and feels formal, formulaic or weak, it probably is.

If your response resonates with you at a heartfelt level, it probably is heartfelt.

Exercise: Gratitude (II)

Appreciation, in its active sense, is the *expression* of that gratitude.

When you know it in your head and feel it in your heart, you are prepared to act — that is, you are prepared to actively express your gratitude to the individual who was instrumental in making it possible.

Now it's time for you to put it all into practice and make it real.

What is one specific contribution that someone in your crew has made recently to your team, group or community and for which you are grateful?

See PDF Worksheet p. 91

Who is the individual?

See PDF Worksheet p. 91

Why are you grateful?

See PDF Worksheet p. 91

Finally, this is an opportunity for you to remind the members of your crew about your larger purpose, as well as to reinforce their place and their contribution. Be prepared to let the individual know how their contribution fits into the bigger picture for your group or community. This is especially important for individuals who might be struggling with the myopia of the routine or the mundane. Your making this effort could help them rediscover and reconnect (pages 186–187).

How does this specific contribution:

Benefit others?

See PDF Worksheet p. 92

Serve the larger group or community?

See PDF Worksheet p. 92

Love lies at the core of all the roles that you will step into as a leader. In the several roles that I will describe in the follow-up to this book, *The Citizen Leader in Action* series, I will refer to love by a host of different and familiar names: caring, enthusiasm, passion . . . Whatever the name, the place of origin is still the same: the heart. You build and strengthen the bonds that move others when you operate from a place of the heart — from a place of love.

Pure and simple, people who love are the better leaders.

YOUR NEXT STEPS

In the months ahead, come back and review the readings, the questions, your writings and your responses in this second part of *The Citizen Leader*. Continue to insist that the content of your character guide your behaviors, your words, your choices and your actions. Embrace the challenge to be an active citizen and an engaging leader in your community — at work and at home, in school and at play, in your neighborhoods and in the world around you. And commit to participate, serve, act and lead, thereby making meaningful contributions and a better life for all.

Here are several specific ongoing activities and actions for you to pursue:

- Champion a cause or take the lead on an initiative that you care about, and that will serve to better your community and improve life for all. Know . . . Care . . . Act!
- Model the force of courage for your peers and members of your community by taking compelling, principle-guided action to advance your initiative.
- If you know someone who is losing their enthusiasm, help them to broaden, rediscover and reconnect.
- If you know someone who is trying to redirect or reinvent, help them to muster their force of courage to follow through.

PERSONAL REFLECTIONS AND LEARNING

When, after some time had passed, the beloved American philosopher and essayist Henry David Thoreau would sit down to dine with a friend or neighbor, he would initiate their reacquaintance by asking, *"What has become clear to you since last we met?"*

I asked you to meet yourself honestly in the first chapter of the book, "Self-Awareness." I asked you to gather data, both from yourself and from others, to discern and detect the qualities that you look for in a citizen and a leader. Then I asked you to consider all that you learned from the data, and state what you believed your strengths were, in light of what you and the people around you sought. Finally, I asked you to be candid with yourself about which qualities you needed or wanted to strengthen, both as a citizen and as a leader.

That exercise in self-awareness launched you on a rigorous internal exploration of your character. Your trajectory brought you to a point where you committed to how you will express your character in your communities and in the world. You read several perspectives that spoke to the proposition that when you live from your core — when you behave, speak and act with integrity — you live a life of meaning.

You examined the essence of active citizenship and read that it is contribution that distinguishes an active citizen. You took steps to make your own contribution to your community: you defined an initiative to champion (know), delved deep into why you personally care to take the lead (care) and proposed impactful actions to move the initiative forward (act).

You read that as you apply your mental resolve (head) with your heartfelt care (heart) to a cause, you courage to act (hands on!) despite fear and risk. And as you engage others to do the same, you hearten them when you feel your gratitude and express your appreciation.

So now, in the spirit of reacquaintance, as well as in the spirit of your meeting yourself anew in these pages, ask yourself: *"What has become clear to me over the course of these chapters?"*

See PDF Worksheet p. 93

To laugh often and love much; to win the respect of intelligent persons and the affection of children; to earn the appreciation of honest citizens and endure the betrayal of false friends; to appreciate beauty; to find the best in others; to give of oneself; to leave the world a bit better, whether by a healthy child, a garden patch or a redeemed social condition; to have played and laughed with enthusiasm and danced with exultation; to know one life has breathed easier because you have lived . . . this is to have succeeded."

— Ralph Waldo Emerson

REVIEW OF QUESTIONS

On the following several pages, you will find all of the essential questions for each chapter of *The Citizen Leader* complied and presented in the same sequential order as they appear in the book. There is one important change: I have recast the questions in the *first* person so that they appeal to you directly. For example, rather than asking the question (as it appears in the book), "What strengths do *you* bring to being a citizen," I have rewritten the question to read, "What strengths do *I* bring to being a citizen?"

Use these questions both to continue to challenge your understanding of and relationship with your values and guiding principles, and to continue to help you apply the frameworks and tools as you participate, serve and lead in your communities.

Part One: Character

1. SELF-AWARENESS
My World and Me
- What are the essential qualities, values or behaviors I look for in a citizen?
- Why do I look for *these* qualities in particular?
- What strengths do I bring to being a citizen?
- What qualities, values or behaviors do I need to *strengthen* as a citizen?
- Why?
- What strengths do I bring to being a leader?
- What qualities, values or behaviors do I need to *strengthen* as a leader?
- Why?

2. CONVICTIONS

Community

- Who are my communities?
- Choose one.
- Who is in this particular community?
- I am an active citizen of _____ community!

  write it here

Convictions

- What are my strong beliefs about this community?
- What are the more significant services or work that *I am doing* in this community?
- I do this service or work because . . .
- I care about my service or work because . . .
- How does my service or work improve life for others?

3. CREDIBILITY

Personal Integrity and Credibility

- What are my promises about how I will conduct myself, both in private and out in the world?
- How consistently do I live up to the promises that I make to myself and to others?
- As I take a look at the work I do or the service I regularly perform in my community, what principles or values does my work or service reflect?
- As I think back on how I chose to spend my time during the last few weeks, what principles or values were reflected in the choices I made about how I spent my time?
- If I were to describe a few interactions I had at work and in my personal life over the past few days, what key principles or values do my interactions seem to demonstrate?
- What are some routine choices I have made over the past few days, even those I made when no one else was looking? What words or concepts most accurately capture the principles or values underlying my choices?

- If I were to put myself in the shoes of some people with whom I interact at work, at home and in regular daily life, what principles and values do I think *others* would say they *regularly* see at play in the ways I behave, talk with others, make choices and generally interact in our community?

Pattern of My Actions

- What principles and values are supported by the *pattern of my actions*?
- What does each value look like day to day by way of my actual behaviors, words and choices?

Guiding Principles Dashboard — Self-Assessment

Guiding Principles Dashboard — Feedback From Others

Growth and Mastery

- How does my self-assessment compare to what others have shared with me?
- What better and fuller understanding do I have about:
  - The character that resides at my core?
  - Who I am in other's eyes?
- What handful of values and principles do I actually demonstrate regularly in my behaviors, words and choices?
- Who or how do I aspire to *be* (that is different from who or how I am today)?
- Why do I care?
- What are my concerns and reservations about whether this is possible?
- What do I need to do in the future to grow in integrity?
- What do I need to do to grow in credibility?

4. LIVING WITH INTEGRITY IN MY COMMUNITY

Values of My Community

- Which one of my communities do I choose?
- What are the values or guiding principles that most accurately describe the way individuals in my community . . .
  - . . . *regularly* behave toward one another?
  - . . . *regularly* speak with one another?

- What are the values or guiding principles that *most frequently* influence . . .
  - . . . the choices people make in our community?
  - . . . the decisions people make?
  - . . . the actions people take?
- Based on my observations and experiences, what do I consider to be the essential *handful* of shared values of my community?
- How do I see each one of these values *regularly* expressed in action?

Living with Integrity

- Which of my guiding principles are most aligned with those of my community?
- Which community values or guiding principles must I make the effort to adhere to more closely to strengthen my bond with my community?
- I care to make the effort because . . .
- What specific behaviors and actions will I demonstrate *regularly (or more regularly)* in order to adhere more closely to these community values?
- Which of my guiding principles are at odds with those of my community?
- Why are they at odds?
- How do I handle it when one (or more) of the shared values of my community seems to be at odds with my guiding principles?

Co-Creator

- Which values or guiding principles must we — the members of the community — strive to adhere to more closely in the next twelve to eighteen months?
- Why is it important for us to adhere more closely to this value?
- Is there any other value or guiding principle that we would be well served to adopt and adhere to in the next twelve to eighteen months?
- Define the value or principle.
- Why is it important for us to adhere to this value?

Strengthen the Character of My Community

- What specific behaviors and actions will I regularly demonstrate so as to support these important community values or guiding principles?
- What specific behaviors and actions will I ask *others* to regularly demonstrate so as to support these important community values or guiding principles?

The Signature By Which I *Will* Be Known

- I am known by these personal guiding principles that I already regularly demonstrate through my actions.
- I aspire to be known by these personal guiding principles and commit to regularly demonstrate them in the future.
- I am and aspire to be known by these community values that I will regularly demonstrate through my actions.
- These are values we would be well served to adopt in our community. I commit to demonstrate them through my actions.

Part Two: Active Citizen

5. CONTRIBUTION

Contribution in Service to My Community (for individuals)

- Who are the people I serve in this community?
- What do I love about the people I serve?
- I am deeply grateful to the people I serve for . . .
- What do I love about the products I offer or the services I perform in this community?
- How do these products or services enrich the lives of the people I serve?
- How would the lives or the experience of those people be diminished if I did not exist?
- What is *my* purpose in my community or my organization?

Contribution in Service to Our Community (for groups)

- Who are the people we serve in this community?
- What do I love about the people we collectively serve?
- I am deeply grateful to the people we serve for . . .
- What do I love about the products we offer or the services we perform?
- How do these products or services enrich the lives of the people we serve?
- How would the lives or the experience of those people be diminished if we did not exist?
- What is *our* purpose as an organization?

6. ACTIVE CITIZENSHIP

Know

- What initiative or change do I want to champion or am I being asked to lead in my community?
- What is one piece of evidence that convinces me of the need for the initiative or change?
- What do I anticipate the obstacles to be to implementing the initiative or change?
- What will be the benefits when the initiative or change is successfully implemented?
- What would be the consequences if it were not implemented?

Care

- I *personally* care about this initiative or change because . . .
- Go deep: I *personally* care about this initiative or change because . . .
- Go deeper: I *personally* care about this initiative or change because . . .

Act

- What are you doing *now* to champion the initiative?
- Is it having an impact?
- Why do you say so? What are the compelling effects?
- What are the possible actions or risks you could take to:
  - champion or lead this change?
  - address the key obstacles?

7. COURAGE

Fears and Risks

- Do I have the necessary *force of courage* to champion the initiative or change that I think is important in my community?
- If I feel that I lack the necessary *force of courage*, whose support can I enlist to help me overcome my reservations and fears? And what will I ask of each of these individuals?

I *courage* to . . .

- What *impactful* principle-guided actions do *I courage to* take in the next three weeks to champion or lead this initiative or change?
- Why *this* action?
- What will be the measure of progress?

Broaden . . . Rediscover . . . Reconnect

- When I look back at my convictions about the people I serve and see how the services or products I provide enrich their lives, what broader perspective about my current endeavors comes into focus?
- What is *my* purpose in my community or my organization?
- How do my daily activities help me fulfill my purpose?
- What is the contribution that my group or organization makes to the lives of all the citizens of the community?
- How does my group or organization's contribution better the lives of others?

Force of Courage to Redirect or Reinvent

- What happens when, with introspection and reflection, I realize that I am acting on behalf of a cause for which I have little passion and have lost my enthusiasm?
- What can I do when my spirit, my sense of self, suffers because the cause no longer gives me much enthusiasm or strength to carry on?

8. ENCOURAGE

Hearten Others

Gratitude is *a feeling I have of being thankful to someone for something.*

On the *giving* end:

Let me recall an occasion when I offered a *meaningful* expression of gratitude to someone.

- Specifically, what occurred, and what did I actually say?
- What was the impact on *me*?

Now, to look at the *receiving* end:

Let me recall an occasion when I received a *meaningful* expression of gratitude.

- Specifically, what occurred, what was said to me and what made it *meaningful?*
- What was the impact on *me?*
- If it was work related, what was the impact on my own work?

Appreciation, in its active sense, is the *expression* I make of the gratitude I feel to another for something.

Let me think back on one specific contribution that someone in my crew recently made to our team, group or community for which I feel personally grateful.

- The individual is . . .
- I feel grateful because . . .

I now realize that this specific contribution . . .

- benefits others, because . . .
- serves the larger group or community in ways such as . . .

Tools

Guiding Principles Dashboard

Name: _____

I would like you to give me some feedback on the strength of my guiding principles and values. In the grid below, I have written the guiding principles and values that I aspire to embody in my everyday behaviors, words and choices.

Please think back on our interactions or your observations of me in the past few weeks.

With what frequency do my behaviors, words and choices *regularly* demonstrate the principles that I have written below? The key is *regularly*.

Seldom	Sometimes	About Half the Time	Often	Almost Always
①	②	③	④	⑤

My Guiding Principles and Values	Behaviors	Words	Choices
EXAMPLE Value: *Diversity* This means: *I include individuals with diverse experiences and knowledge on my projects.* *I actively seek out differing points of view before making important choices.* *I insist on and support the members of my group for doing the same.*	4	5	3
Value: This means:			

Copyright © 2011 by Bridge Group Communications, LLC. All rights reserved.

Name: _____

Seldom	**Sometimes**	**About Half the Time**	**Often**	**Almost Always**
①	②	③	④	⑤

My Guiding Principles and Values	Behaviors	Words	Choices
Value: This means:			
Value: This means:			
Value: This means:			
Value: This means:			

Copyright © 2011 by Bridge Group Communications, LLC. All rights reserved.

Name: _____

On a separate page, please answer the following questions for each score of below 4 that you marked on the dashboard:

1. Why did you not give a score of 4 or 5?
2. What would I need to be doing differently for you to raise the score to a 4 or a 5?

Finally, please let me know if there are any *other* principles — good, bad or indifferent — that you would say *regularly* guide the ways in which I behave, talk with others, make choices and generally interact with you and others in the community.

Please return no later than _____
write in date

Return information:

Thank you for your participation and candor. I'm very grateful.

Copyright © 2011 by Bridge Group Communications, LLC. All rights reserved.

Community Values Dashboard

This *Community Values Dashboard* will help you assess the strength of your:

1. engagement with your community values and
2. adherence to those values.

You can measure the strength of your personal *engagement* by assessing both:

- the degree to which you really **know** what each value means (gauged by how clearly you can explain its meaning to someone else) and
- the degree to which you say that you **care** about and support the value.

You can measure the strength of your personal *adherence* to the values by assessing:

- the degree to which you **act** in ways that regularly demonstrate the value.

On the grid that follows, assess honestly how much you agree with each of these three statements:

- Know: I can clearly explain the meaning of this value to someone else in our community.
- Care: I personally care about and support this value.
- Act: My behaviors, words and actions *regularly* demonstrate this value. The key word is *regularly*.

Copyright © 2011 by Bridge Group Communications, LLC. All rights reserved.

Strongly Disagree ①	Disagree ②	Neutral ③	Agree ④	Strongly Agree ⑤

Our Community Values	Know	Care	Act
EXAMPLE Value: *We appreciate and look out for one another.*	4	5	3
Value:			
Value:			
Value:			
Value:			
Value:			

Copyright © 2011 by Bridge Group Communications, LLC. All rights reserved.

On a separate page, please answer the following questions for each score of below 4 that you marked on the dashboard:

1. Why did you not give a score of 4 or 5?
2. What would you need to do differently to raise the score to a 4 or a 5?

Copyright © 2011 by Bridge Group Communications, LLC. All rights reserved.

GREAT READING

I have been instructed and inspired by a wide range of authors, educators, poets, philosophers and professionals as a student, a teacher, a writer and as a human being trying to find my voice and my way in the world. The following is a collection of some of the great reading that has informed my ideas and shaped the spirit of this book.

You will find an online link to each one of these books and published articles at www.TheCitizenLeader.com.

Books about Personal Growth

The Answer to How is Yes
Peter Block
Berrett-Koehler Publishers, Inc., San Francisco, 2002

Care of the Soul: A Guide to Cultivating Depth and Sacredness in Everyday Life
Thomas Moore
HarperCollins Publishers, New York, 1992

The Emperor's Handbook
Marcus Aurelius
New translation of *Meditations*, by C. Scott Hicks and David V. Hicks
Scribner, New York, 2002

Ethics for the New Millennium
His Holiness the Dalai Lama
Riverhead Books, New York, 1999

First You Have to Row a Little Boat: Reflections on Life and Living
Richard Bode
Warner Books, New York, 1993

The Heart Aroused: Poetry and the Preservation of Soul in Corporate America
David Whyte
Doubleday, New York, 1994

Instructions to the Cook: A Zen Master's Lessons in Living a Life That Matters
Bernard Glassman and Rick Fields
Bell Tower, New York, 1996

A Joseph Campbell Companion: Reflections on the Art of Living
Diane Osbon
HarperCollins, New York, 1991

Letters to a Young Poet
Rainer Maria Rilke
W. W. Norton & Company, New York, 1934

Mastery: The Keys to Success and Long-Term Fulfillment
George Leonard
Plume, New York, 1992

The Measure of Our Success: A Letter to My Children and Yours
Marian Wright Edelman
HarperPerennial, New York, 1993

Orbiting the Giant Hairball: A Corporate Fool's Guide to Surviving with Grace
Gordon MacKenzie
Viking Penguin, New York, 1998

The Road Less Traveled
M. Scott Peck
Simon and Schuster, New York, 1978

Soul of a Citizen: Living with Conviction in a Cynical Time
Paul Rogat Loeb
St. Martin's Griffin, New York, 1999

Tuesdays with Morrie: An Old Man, A Young Man, and Life's Greatest Lessons
Mitch Albom
Doubleday, New York, 1997

Where I Lived, and What I Lived For
Henry David Thoreau
Penguin Books, 2006

Books, Biographies and Stories about Leadership and Community

Authentic Leadership: Rediscovering the Secrets of Creating Lasting Value
Bill George
Jossey-Bass Publishers, San Francisco, 2003

Built to Last: Successful Habits of Visionary Companies
Jim Collins and Jerry I. Porras
HarperCollins Publishers, 1994

Credibility: How Leaders Gain and Lose It, Why People Demand It
James Kouzes and Barry Posner
Jossey-Bass Publishers, San Francisco, 1993

Encouraging the Heart: A Leader's Guide to Rewarding and Recognizing Others
James M. Kouzes and Barry Z. Posner
Jossey-Bass Publishers, San Francisco, 2003

Finding Flow: The Psychology of Engagement with Everyday Life
Mihaly Csikszentmihalyi
Basic Books, 1998

Greater Than Yourself: The Ultimate Lesson of True Leadership
Steve Farber
Doubleday, New York, 2009

The Hungry Spirit: Beyond Capitalism: A Quest for Purpose in the Modern World
Charles Handy
Broadway Books, 1998

The Leadership Challenge, 4th Edition
James M. Kouzes and Barry Z. Posner
Jossey-Bass Publishers, San Francisco, 2008

The Leader of the Future 2: Visions, Strategies, and Practices for the New Era
Frances Hesselbein and Marshall Goldsmith, editors
Jossey-Bass Publishers, San Francisco, September 2006

Leading Out Loud: Inspiring Change Through Authentic Communications,
New and Revised
Terry Pearce
Jossey-Bass Publishers, San Francisco, 2003

Let My People Go Surfing: The Education of a Reluctant Businessman
Yvon Chouinard
The Penguin Press, New York, 2005

PEAK: How Great Companies Get Their Mojo from Maslow
Chip Conley
Jossey-Bass Publishers, San Francisco, 2007

The Political Ecology of the Modern Peasant: Calculation and Community
Leslie Anderson
The Johns Hopkins University Press, 1994

Profiles in Courage
John Fitzgerald Kennedy
HarperCollins, New York, 1956

The Radical Leap Re-Energized
Steve Farber
No Limit Publishing, Tempe, AZ, 2011

Working with Emotional Intelligence
Dan Goleman
Bantam, New York, 1998

Periodicals and Published Articles

Online Articles

The Hidden Qualities of Great Leaders
James Champy
FastCompany, November 2003

Soft Skills, High Impact on the Leadership Track
Deborah Solomon Reid
Tuck Today, Summer 2003

Take the Hit: The Breakfast of Champions and Great Leaders
Mark Goulston
FastCompany, September 2006

What Makes Leaders Great
Tricia Bisoux
BizEd Magazine, September–October 2005

Harvard Business Review — Essential Reading

The Discipline of Building Character
John Badaracco Jr.
Harvard Business Review, March–April 1998, Reprint 98201

The Hard Work of Being a Soft Manager
William H. Peace
Harvard Business Review, December 2001, Reprint R0111G

Level 5 Leadership
Jim Collins
Harvard Business Review, January–February 2001, Reprint R0101D

Primal Leadership: The Hidden Driver of Great Performance
D. Goldman, R. Boyatzis and A. McKee
Harvard Business Review, December 2001, Reprint R0111C

Why Should Anyone Be Led By You?
Robert Goffee and Gareth Jones
Harvard Business Review, September–October 2000, Reprint RO0506

Please check back online, from time to time, for additions to this list of Great Reading.

ABOUT THE AUTHOR

Peter Alduino is president and founder of Bridge Group Communications, LLC.

He brings 20 years of experience and insight working, learning and teaching in the fields of leadership and management development to the design, content and facilitation of *The Citizen Leader*. The mission for this and all his work is to help those who are, or aspire to be, leaders to build strong bonds with the members of their organizations and communities so that together they can accomplish their worthy goals.

Peter's sense of mission is driven by his strong desire to help his clients enrich their own lives, while also creating great places to live, work and play. He is guided by these, his personal and professional values: dare to be true, do good work in service of the common good, honor others, be fair and make choices that promote a healthy mind, body and spirit.

Earlier in Life

Before founding Bridge Group Communications, Peter held the position of Principal with The Tom Peters Group, during which time he conducted leadership development seminars worldwide based on the research and writing of thought leaders in the field, including colleagues Terry Pearce, author of *Leading Out Loud*; and Jim Kouzes and Barry Posner, authors of *The Leadership Challenge, Credibility, Encouraging the Heart* and *A Leader's Legacy*.

For five years, Peter was a lecturer in Leadership Communication for M.B.A. students at the University of California, Berkeley, in the Walter A. Haas School of Business.

His first career was in investment banking in Boston.

Peter holds an M.B.A. from the Amos Tuck School of Business Administration at Dartmouth College, a B.A. *magna cum laude* from Bowdoin College and the C.P.L.F. *1er Degré* from Université de Paris–Sorbonne (Paris IV).

The Henry Luce Foundation named him a 1980 Luce Scholar.

A Balanced Life

Peter lives in Santa Cruz, California. When he is not working with clients or writing, he can often be found outdoors relishing the natural beauty of the central California coast.

GRATITUDE

A wise and learned mentor has said to me on a number of occasions, "We all stand on the shoulders of giants." And so, I would like to begin my acknowledgments by offering sincere thanks to the giants whose thought leadership, words of encouragement and friendship have inspired me and given me the confidence and the courage to pursue the thinking and writing that has resulted in *The Citizen Leader*. To Jim Kouzes, Terry Pearce and Steve Farber, I extend my enduring gratefulness. This book was born out of my desire to contribute to the chorus of voices, like yours, that strive to enrich the lives of individuals who aspire to speak with authenticity, act with principle and serve as a positive force in the world.

I am indebted to the many colleagues, clients, scholars and writers whose professional experiences, experiments (both successes and failures), research, common sense, courage, kindness and wisdom have influenced my ideas. In my life I have encountered writers, artists, philosophers, poets and everyday people whose words have inspired my writing. I have tried to acknowledge and credit them all along the way.

Writing *The Citizen Leader* has also been a journey of self-discovery. While composing every question, I asked each one of myself to weigh whether it made sense, to gauge whether it resonated with me and to assess whether and what I could learn. As a result, I've grown in self-awareness, matured in my emotional hardiness and deepened in my sense of personal integrity. I have also been prompted, indeed carried along the way at moments, by the wisdom of the great American philosophers Ralph Waldo Emerson and Henry David Thoreau, frequently cited in these pages, who challenged me to "be true to myself . . . and to my work." I have been bolstered by the motto of my high school, Milton Academy, which so wonderfully impressed on me the imperative to "dare to be true." And I have always felt challenged by the call of my college, Bowdoin, to "serve the common good" — a call that offers both reason and hope for this work.

My Uncle Anthony, whose thoughts I have shared several times in these pages, believed deeply that my work could benefit you. His generosity in the final years of his life allowed me to devote a good part of my time to turning *The Citizen Leader*® seminars into these self-guided books to share with you. He was a worrier, but today I can say to him, though he has departed this life, "Now we have no problem."

An old Japanese expression says, "It takes two knives to keep one sharp." I would like to acknowledge and extend my sincere appreciation to Sharon Landes and LJ Rose, who have acted as that other knife for me and have helped me sharpen the content of *The Citizen Leader* over the past few years. Sharon and LJ, you have prompted me to think deeply. You have given me valuable feedback on the philosophy and content of the material. And you have kept me at the top of my game. Thank you.

I extend my deep gratitude to my editor, Karen Leland. It was some twenty years ago that you and I met, and that you got me launched on this trajectory. At critical junctures ever since, and quite unexpectedly, our paths have crossed. And each time, your generous counsel has prompted me to make choices and take directions that have greatly enriched my life.

Joe Wert, thank you for taking a leap of faith on the guy in cowboy boots, giving me a new start in the West and being a fine mentor.

I thank Daniel Voskoboynikov, the twenty-something co-owner of the local Harbor Cafe in Santa Cruz who leads a crew of fifteen or so. When I shared with him that I wrote and taught seminars on leadership development, he asked me, "Gee, do you have anything *I* could read?" I started writing this self-guided version of *The Citizen Leader*® seminars the very next day.

For months thereafter, my writing was fueled by a morning americano brewed by the folks at People's Coffee. Thanks to Curtis, Austin and all the others.

I extend my heartfelt gratitude to Lauren Crux, who prompted me to finish this work with the reminder, "Don't let perfect get in the way of good."

Thank you to my early readers Eli Orlic, Diana Vicari and Chip Conley. Your generosity, both in time and feedback, helped me shape a much better work for future readers. And thank you to the talented crew of professionals and artists who endeavored to perfect the pages that I gave them, by their keen attention to detail and design: copyeditor Mark Woodworth, designers CJ de Heer and Michele DeFilippo and the team at 1106 Design, photographer Chris Schmauch, and ebook conversion designer Joshua Tallent at Ebook Architects.

Finally and foremost, I express my heartfelt thanks to my partner, CJ, for your love, your patience and your words of encouragement (*"I'm very proud of what you have created"*) at each step along the way. You have been there to provide moral and emotional support. You have challenged my thinking, read every page and helped me flesh out my thoughts. *The Citizen Leader* is a better work for your attention. Thank you for your invaluable contribution to helping me do good work in service of the common good.

Peter Alduino
Santa Cruz, California

August 2011

CPSIA information can be obtained at www.ICGtesting.com
Printed in the USA
BVOW081137081111

275594BV00002B/9/P